ESSEX

A COUNTY HISTORY

Stan Jarvi

D1227024

COUNTRYSIDE BOOKS

NEWBURY, BERKSHIRE

First Published 1993
© Stan Jarvis 1993

COUNTRYSIDE BOOKS
3 Catherine Road
Newbury, Berkshire

ISBN 1 85306 245 6

The engraving on the title page is
dated 1791, and shows the north west
view of Colchester Castle.

The cover photograph is of Thaxted from the air
and was taken by Edward Clack.

Designed by Mon Mohan
Produced through MRM Associates Ltd., Reading
Printed in England by J.W. Arrowsmith Ltd., Bristol

Contents

Acknowledgements

Photographs in this book have been used with the kind permission of the following: Edward Clack, pages 8, 9, 15, 42, 62, 65, 79, 93, 94, 101, 120, 146, 177; Essex County Council, pages 43, 153; Chelmsford and Essex Museum, pages 21, 157; Colchester Museum, pages 31, 32; Colchester Archaeological Trust, page 35; Mike Bonser, page 45; Essex Chronicle, pages 50, 51, 69, 112, 147, 168; London Borough of Barking and Dagenham, page 64; Essex Review, page 83; Chelmsford Library, page 160; The Essex Regiment Museum, page 167; Ford Company Ltd, page 173; Capital and Counties PLC, page 183; Dartford River Crossing Ltd and Trafalgar House Construction Ltd, page 185; Harlow District Council, page 180; Mark Mitchels, page 67. My thanks also to The Council for British Archaeology, and to Tim Green for his help with the maps.

I am grateful to them all for their interest and help in the illustration of this book.

Introduction

The famous novelist Sylvia Townsend Warner (1893–1978) observed that 'The events of history carry a certain exhilaration with them' and Essex is a county which has experienced that exhilaration, and its antithesis despair, through the chapters of its long story. Essex saw the Romans make its ruler-straight roads, the Saxons define its boundaries and the Normans install its aristocracy. It was the cockpit for the cruelties of the Peasants' Revolt and the witchcraft trials and it witnessed the gaudy 'progresses' of kings and queens on pleasure bent throughout the county. In more modern times Essex people cheered Queen Victoria as she opened Epping Forest to the public at large and welcomed Queen Elizabeth II when she opened the great bridge named after her which now spans the Thames.

There is so much material available from which to outline the County's progress through the years that the aspiring historian's main problem is how to cram into a book of readable length a representative selection of the exciting events in which countless generations of Essex people have been involved. My book is offered as the entrance hall to a great house of history. I have tried to show the character of Essex as it melded into a corporate, English identity.

In my efforts I have been helped by so many people, of whom I would especially like to thank the following: the staff of the Chelmsford and Colchester libraries, the Essex Record Office and the Archaeological, Highways and Information departments of Essex County Council; the *Essex Chronicle* and the *Essex County Standard*, and the Council for British Archaeology. Without the help of friends like Ron Patient and John Candlin, I could not have contemplated such an undertaking. Organisations which have been kind enough to answer my requests for illustrations are mentioned in the captions. This is the fifth book of mine published by Nicholas and Suzanne Battle. I would like to thank them and Amanda Smith for the way in which they turn my much-corrected manuscripts into finished books of such pleasing design.

Last, and most important, my wife Hazel has supported me throughout the gestation of this book, offering encouragement, practical help and advice. Without her sympathy and understanding it would not have been completed. To Hazel, with love, I dedicate this book.

1

WHAT MAKES ESSEX

A county's history through 10,000 years must be influenced by its physical features and the underlying structure of its land. So it is with Essex. A bird's eye view shows Essex sloping gently from the north west to the south eastern coast, as if preparing to slide slowly into the North Sea. Millions of years ago, Essex, along with the rest of Britain, lay at the bottom of the sea, where the chalk beds that underlie the county's boulder clay and gravel layers of subsoil, were formed.

The land we see today can be summed up like this: to the north west of the county, roughly from Roydon through Chelmsford to Colchester, there is a plateau of boulder clay, mixed in some places with chalk. The ancient deposit of chalk still comes to the surface at Saffron Walden in the north west and at Grays to the south east. This chalk has been worked for man's needs since prehistoric times. At Thurrock on the north bank of the Thames it is worked in quarries associated with the great cement factory which was such a landmark, with its smoke-belching chimneys seen by all who travelled by the Purfleet–Dartford tunnel. The Dene Holes in Thurrock show how ancient man burrowed his way down into the chalk, forming caverns in his search for flints from which to make his tools.

Under the boulder clay lies the gravel – rocks broken down by glacial action and pushed down from the north. It forms a rumpled blanket yards deep, surfacing and diving deep under clay and sand and loam. Another valuable deposit left by the action of glaciers and their melt water is the brick earth found in pockets all over the county. It is sufficiently near the surface, and in such quantities in some places, to sustain large local brick and tile industries between the Stour and the Colne and on the banks of the Chelmer, Blackwater, Crouch, Roach and Thames. Such earth is also very fertile, supporting plentiful crops since man first farmed it.

The larger rivers find their outlets in the boulder-clay plateau and run with the inclined plane, the lie of the land, from north west to south east.

Any motorist driving down to the Thames from the north will notice the ridge from which there is an unusual lofty view of the Thames and the Kent countryside. Beyond, it can suddenly open up before the abrupt drop to the Thameside towns and villages. This 'scarp', not high, but steep, extends as far as the eye can see on either side. The explanation is that this was once the northern bank of an altogether mightier Thames, made unimaginably vast when the melting glaciers of the Ice Age caused the river to bend northeast-wards in its course, to join the Rhine and flow on north into a northern ocean long before our North Sea came into being. The formation of the marshlands along the Essex coast up to the low cliffs of Harwich gives credence to this theory.

By and large, the residents in the thousands of homes on estates built since the Second World War, find themselves tilling the obstinate London Clay which, when it is broken down and fertilised can make an excellent growing medium. Farmers on the 'three-horseland', the stiff blue London Clay which weathers brown, sticky and glue-like, found it almost impossible to work until the advent of mechanisation. In wet weather it made the ill-clad agricultural labourer's life a misery. It covers the south, the east and west of the county, and is interspersed with alluvial soil on river banks.

People living on the tumbled debris of the ancient glacier paths enjoy a medium soil, but the jagged flints and the broken gravel, together with the rounded pebbles, make cultivation more difficult. Farmers have broken many a tine and blade on the obdurate stones which can be of all sizes and from rock strata hundreds of miles from their original source, moved on and down by glaciers. Central north eastern Essex is covered in this manner. One place in Essex – Ingatestone – even gets its name from the vast conglomerate of rock called pudding stone which marked a prehistoric track, used possibly by early salt traders. Later Saxon settlers made their homes here, and as pioneers passed on through to new sites for settlement they called this place the 'Ing' or people, at the Stone. In another place, Dedham, a great boulder can be seen in the churchyard on the south side of the church. In 1907 an old man told the story of this huge boulder, a leftover from the Ice Age, and it was written down for posterity. Edward Ward, a ploughman, had the plough almost jerked from his hands as it hit an obstruction under the soil. He tried to dig it out but it was too large to excavate in work time. He set himself to uncover it after he had finished work, then asked the farmer if he could use his tackle to take it to his cottage. He let it be known to all his relations that this great boulder was to be his and his wife's gravestone. His wish was faithfully observed, but the relatives did not have that stone inscribed. So the humble ploughman and his wife

The Church of The Holy Innocents at High Beech, in Epping Forest, a small part of a once great forest that covered the county.

lie anonymously beneath a stone which will outlast the finest monument in the churchyard.

The chalk soils on the north west border of the county are thin and dry. The earliest settlers sited their crude huts on the patches of glacial drift and gravel where there was a better water supply.

Stone Age people were settled in Essex some 7,500 years ago, though their simple way of life made no impact on the wilderness that then was Essex. Humans made themselves thoroughly at home in Essex, living off the forested land and the creatures it supported.

The all-pervading forest had, by about 5,000 BC, diversified to include oak, ash, beech, elm, lime and other varieties as we see them today in those relatively tiny enclaves at Epping and Hatfield – the last, and now zealously guarded, relics of the Great Forest of Essex. Formerly the forest pressed down to the foreshore and clothed the banks of the rivers. Those rivers were the natural highways for the people from the Stone Age right through to modern times when they were canalised to take even more advantage of nature's easy access to the heart of the county.

There are at least 22 rivers and streams in Essex significant enough to have been named by our Saxon forefathers. Four main rivers form its ancient boundaries. The Thames forms the 35-mile south border, although it does not drain any part of the county directly except through its tributaries the Lea, the Roding, the Ingrebourne and some minor streams. Down the western side of the county runs the Lea which, having taken the waters of the Stort at Roydon, continues on its southward way to the Thames. The Lea has formed the boundary of the county since AD 886 when King Alfred negotiated with the Danish ruler Guthrum that all the land east of the river should remain under Danelaw while the other bank would form the extent of Alfred's kingdom of Mercia. The Stort rises on the border of Essex with Hertfordshire, between Langley in the former and Nuthampstead in the latter. It acts as the county border for a couple of miles, then wanders into Essex through Clavering, Manuden and Birchanger to Stansted Mountfitchet, where it again forms the border for a mile or so. After another meander for a couple of miles it once again forms the border down to the Lea at Roydon, though it does wander away west of the Hallingbury villages.

Our county's northern border is defined by the Stour. Forty three of its 52-mile long course traces the county's outline. Having risen near Brinkley in Suffolk, it flows south east to arrive on the Essex border at Sturmer. Once there was a great lake here and the Stour mere gave the settlement its name of Sturmere, as shown in the Domesday Book.

The Stour was first made navigable for small trading ships, from Sudbury down to its mouth, in 1712 or thereabouts. An improved navigation 24 miles long with 15 locks was opened in 1796. The barges were pulled by two horses upstream and one coming down. The journey between Sudbury and Mistley on the estuary took twelve hours. Upstream, another two hours were needed. The towpath crossed the river 32 times and the horses were trained to cross by jumping on and off the bows of the barge. Whereas other canal companies had bought the riparian rights to the land needed for towpaths, the Stour Navigation Company was content to lease such land so, when it closed down, the river banks reverted to the riverside farmers – and that is why there are few public walks beside the Stour to this day. At Mistley the Stour, rapidly widening into a tidal estuary, can accommodate coasters up to a thousand tons burthen. By the time it joins the Orwell to form Harwich Harbour some ten miles on, it takes vessels of up to 15,000 tons which operate out of Britain's second largest passenger ferry terminal.

The Chelmer rises in Rowney Wood, Debden, some 370 feet above sea level and runs for 35 miles from west of Thaxted through the Easton villages, the Dunmows, Great and Little, Barnston, Felsted, the Walthams, Broomfield, Springfield and Chelmsford – the county town from which the river gained its name. But it is actually the Can which runs through the town centre and under the old Stone Bridge. The Chelmer cuts across under the Springfield Road and then meets its fate as the terminus of the Chelmer and Blackwater Navigation, with wharves and

An aerial view of Thaxted. Its gently rolling pastures, beyond the little market, would once have been well-wooded. The town's guildhall shows the timber framing practised by Essex craftsmen from the earliest times.

warehouses built to unload and store the goods brought up by barge from Heybridge Basin, where the sea-going ships tied up.

The Chelmer was still technically a river, for it continued to drive many a mill wheel on loops of the river which had to be bypassed by the canal engineers. So the river runs on, with canalised stretches, through Boreham and Baddow, Woodham Walter and Ulting, Langford and Maldon to its ultimate 'harbour' at the last lock on the Blackwater estuary. The canal is no longer used other than as a mooring and pleasure boat facility.

The Blackwater rises at Debden very close indeed to the source of the Chelmer. It is called the Pant down to Kings Bridge in Bocking and thereafter is known as the Blackwater right down to the wide Blackwater estuary where the Colne and the Chelmer contribute their waters. After passing through villages from Radwinter to Wethersfield and on to Bocking, the young Pant becomes the adult Blackwater, running on through Coggeshall, Feering, the Braxteds and Wickham Bishops to Langford and a junction with a canalised section of the Chelmer. Here its waters swell the flow which, from 1797, carried a continual procession of barges up and down the last 'cut' taking the canal down to Heybridge Basin.

The Colne, 32 miles long with an extra tidal stretch of seven miles, rises near the back entrance to Moyns Park, Birdbrook at a height of some 300 feet above sea level and flows straightforwardly south east through Colchester. At Great Yeldham, about four miles from its source, it is reinforced by a stream from Stambourne; then it continues on its direct course through the Hedinghams, Halstead, the Colne villages, Lexden and, of course, its great namesake Colchester. On it goes in broadened estuarine form to Wivenhoe and Brightlingsea, where it combines at last with the Blackwater to form that very wide estuary which takes in the Chelmer. It then washes round the islands of Osea, Northey and Mersea and runs at last into the North Sea.

Other rivers which make jagged edges to the outline of Essex include the Crouch and the Roach. The Crouch rises just south of Billericay and runs some 24 miles eastwards through Wickford and Runwell to Battlesbridge where, at high tide, it becomes navigable down the 16 miles of an estuary that widens to a mile and a half between Holliwell Point to the north and Foulness Point to the south. One of its tributaries is the Roch, or Broomhill River, better known today as the Roach. From a source of several springs on high ground east of Rayleigh, it combines as one river near Rochford and flows on eastward to join the Crouch after feeding Potton Creek and the Middleway at Potton Point. The strange thing is that its estuary is twice as long as its course – demonstrating how the coastal valleys were filled by glacial melt in those times.

The Roding runs down to a creek off the Thames; '. . . the insalubrious Barking Creek', as Marcus Crouch puts it. From a source at Chapel End, Broxted, this humble river runs 35 miles through Takeley, the Canfields, the Rodings, Fyfield, the Ongars, the Staplefords, Woodford and Wanstead before it finds the Thames. John Norden, the mapmaker, put it so neatly in 1594: 'The Roding firste appeareth nere Takeley; whence, as she passeth, she greeteth her nine daughters, all the Rodinges.' He was referring to the nine villages then existing that were named after the river: Abbess, Aythorpe, Beauchamp, Berners, High, Leaden, Margaret, Morrells and White Roding.

The Rom, another tributary of the Thames, was known in the past as the Bourne or the Beam. It rises near Brook House, Navestock, and runs south under Bourne Bridge, Stapleford Abbotts, on to its

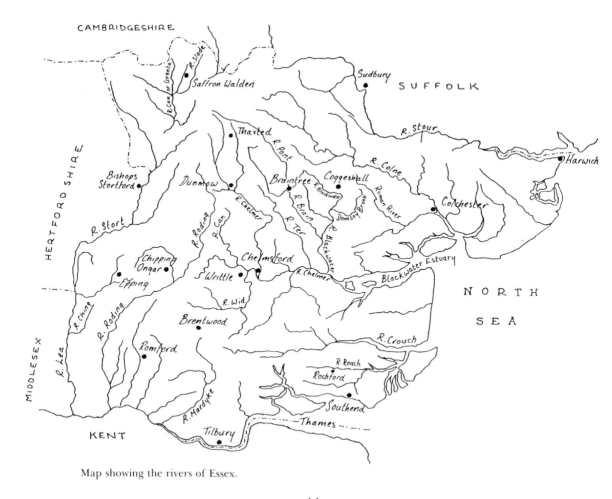

Map showing the rivers of Essex.

namesake Romford and thus directly into the Thames, forming on its way the boundaries of the old parishes of Dagenham and Hornchurch. A perambulation of the Forest of Essex in 1301 states that the Rom formed its eastern boundary '. . . which water runs down from a certain place called Dakenhambeem and from that place by a certain ditch called Maredike between Havering [Liberty] and Dakenham, as far as the line of the water of the Thames.' Just about a mile from the rising of the Rom there springs the Ingrebourne, flowing south to feed the Thames at Rainham, 11 miles away. The Mardyke mentioned in that ancient perambulation is the spring that feeds the lake in Thorndon Park, East Horndon, and runs on ten miles through Childerditch, Bulphan, Orsett and Stifford to join the Thames at Purfleet.

There is often confusion concerning the Cam and the Can. Let us take the Cam first. It rises on that same watershed near Wimbish where four other Essex rivers are born – the Blackwater, the Chelmer, the Roding and the Pincey Brook. The Cam, whose source is between Debden and Henham, has the distinction of being the only river which rises in Essex and flows out of it. After 11 miles through Essex it runs on for another 54 miles to be a tributary of the Great Ouse as it heads for the Wash.

The Can's source is at High Roding. It waters a particularly beautiful vale of villages including Aythorpe Roding, High Easter, Good Easter, Mashbury, Chignall Smealey, Chignall St James, Roxwell and Writtle. So it arrives in the county town where it delivers a considerable volume to the Chelmer. It is itself enriched by the waters of the Wid which runs round three parts of a circle in its 14-mile journey from Blackmore.

The name of the Brain is comparatively modern. It has been traced back to the 13th century, when Braintree was known as Great Rayne in contradistinction to Little Rayne – now known simply as Rayne. Before the river reached Braintree it was always, and still is, known as Pod's Brook – only as it leaves the town is it recognised as the Brain. Taking the river as a whole, it runs 14 miles from south west of Bardfield, near Long Green through Great Saling, Rayne and Braintree, curving north to water the Notley villages and Faulkbourne on its way to Witham and marriage with the Blackwater.

The little Ter rises at Porter's Hall in Stebbing and flows for 15 miles through Felsted, Great and Little Leighs, Feering, Terling and Hatfield Peverel to its meeting with the Chelmer at Ulting. This river was the subject of accusation and investigation during the terrible typhoid fever outbreak in Terling in November 1867. Over six weeks 300 people contracted the disease and 44 died. Its severity brought the situation to the notice of the national press including the *Times* and the *Lancet*.

The Roman River, 11 miles long, rises about a mile west of Tey-brook

Farm at Great Tey. It flows serpent-like south east through Copford and Birch, passes Abberton and Fingringhoe and joins the Colne almost at its mouth. Early writers believed it got its name from the many evidences of Roman occupation of the land it waters, but later authorities, like P H Reaney, show how both river and creek were named after the owners of the land in the 14th century – the Romayn family.

There are other streams and rivulets which have been the reason for settlement by humans in prehistoric times. They may not make much of a contribution to the landscape, but just a moment of reflection on the bank of a small stream like the Roxwell Brook brings to mind the generations of people who have been grateful for its water – the water of life for simple folk scraping a living off the land through 5,000 years or more.

The shape of the county on its seaward side is extremely complex. The endless erosion of the salt marshes by the sea, long before sea walls were raised, combined with silt carried out to sea by all those rivers in flood, created tide-washed sandbanks which stretched more than 20 miles out to sea in some places. The low cliffs to the north east are the county's only defiant gesture to North Sea storms, and they have been made to suffer for it. The old villages of Frinton and Walton were washed away completely by the 18th century. Harwich was once under the direst threat of encirclement by the sea, as will be explained later in the book.

Erosion of the Naze cliff at Walton, particularly in the 'Red Crag' stratum, constantly brings to light fresh layers of fossil remains of mammoth and rhinoceros, shark and shellfish, that enjoyed life in the tropical climate which blessed the land and sea before the Ice Age.

Though a journey distance by sea from Southend direct to Harwich would be no more than 45 miles, the extent of the sea walls needed to keep the sea from inundating the Essex coast would stretch up to four times that distance, so long and wide are the creeks and estuaries which make up the Essex shoreline.

The maritime history of Essex is as varied as its coastline. The shallows and the sandbanks stretching far to sea created a maze of death for sailing ships and denied the county a major port from the mouth of the Thames right up to Harwich. Of course, there were ports where the essentials of life were landed and certain local exports loaded, and where fishing fleets could find safe haven. Barking had a huge fishing fleet sailing regularly out of the Thames; Leigh was a considerable fishing port with general trade from overseas, sufficient to require the establishment there of a custom house. Burnham and Battlesbridge had their quays, the former going on to be an international yachting centre. Maldon was an early and important port until the silting up of the Blackwater reduced the draught which the larger vessels needed. Colchester was a very busy port in the 18th century when its cloth trade was booming, but it lost much of that trade with the onset of the industrial revolution when the new railway system allowed easy distribution from the vast complex of London docks.

The port of Harwich was important from the earliest times, with its ferry service to the continent. Its value was summed up in a report to the Admiralty in 1843: 'Although the rivers Thames and Humber afford shelter by running far up them, yet Harwich, from its easy access by night or day, in all weathers, at all states of the tide, is the only harbour of refuge . . . on the East Coast of England . . .'

The little ports down the Colne – Wivenhoe, Rowhedge, Brightlingsea – were surprisingly prosperous at the turn of the century from the flowering of the yacht-building and repairing activity carried on there. This industry grew to international importance and gave rise to the facilities for large fleets of fishing smacks which were based there.

All sailors heading for Essex ports had to be very careful when threading their way through the sandbanks and the islands. Of the latter there are more than 30 included in the Essex boundaries. Quite a few of them have now been connected to the mainland by causeways. Some are permanent, like the Strood that leads to Mersea; some are tidal, like the raised roads that allow low-tide access to Osea and to Northey.

Canvey Island, now firmly tied to South Benfleet with concrete roads and bridges, is a history book in itself, built up from nothing more than a shifting mudbank in the Thames by the ingenuity of the Dutch engineer Cornelius Vermuyden in 1623. The whole story is laid out to view in the Dutch Cottage Museum on the island. Northey Island saw the Danes encamped before their victory at the Battle of Maldon in AD 991. Mersea Island heard the tramp of Roman troops nearly 1,000 years before that, and Osea Island was used in modern times as a rehabilitation centre for chronic alcoholics. Every island has its story, right down to little Rushley Island. It was just three acres of mud washed by the highest tides as they swept up the creek between Havengore and Wakering Stairs when it was bought for £40 in 1785 or thereabouts. It was walled around and farmed to produce a profit of no less than £330 a year in 1790, and that was a considerable sum in those days. It was overwhelmed by a freak tide in 1791 which bankrupted its owner, John Harriot, the famous progenitor of the Thames River Police. It was later re-walled and is still farmed today. These facts serve simply as representative examples of the importance in the Essex story of its veritable archipelago.

By including in this history the whole area of Essex as it existed up to 1965 and the artificial formation of the Greater London Council, we are following in the footsteps of Essex County Council itself, for it states in a recent copy of its *County Handbook*:

'. . . although the London Boroughs of Barking, Havering, Newham, Redbridge and Waltham Forest, with a population of nearly 1,250,000 are referred to in this book, the Essex mostly dealt with in these pages is a county covering 1,450 square miles and with a population of 1,314,680 . . .'

The towns and villages swallowed up by those new London Boroughs include some really important old Essex settlements; from Walthamstow, Wanstead, West Ham and Leyton eastwards through Ilford, Barking and Dagenham to Havering-atte-Bower, Romford, Hornchurch and Upminster. Even little Cranham achieved fame as the home of General James Oglethorpe, colonial pioneer and prison reformer, who founded the state of Georgia, USA.

In 1965, then, these ancient places left Essex in terms of local government boundaries; but for all the new names and the different divisions between capital and county there are still hundreds of

An aerial view of Mersea Island, one of more than 30 islands included in the Essex boundaries. Mersea Island's causeway, The Strood, was a natural phenomenon developed by the Romans, who inhabited the island from the earliest days of their invasion in 43AD.

thousands of inhabitants of these former Essex villages who identify strongly with the old county. In 1974, there was a big reorganisation of local government within the county, when rural district councils were abolished. Southend-on-Sea lost its status as a County Borough and altogether larger districts were formed. Take the county town as an example; Chelmsford had been incorporated as a Borough in 1888. In 1974 that status was done away with and 27 villages all around the town, formerly administered by the Rural District Council were added to the borough to make the area of the Chelmsford District Council. The office of Mayor was declared redundant and a Chairman presided over council meetings. Later the Chelmsford District Council took up the option to re-introduce the title of Mayor and so preserve a valuable ceremonial link with the past.

That ancient division of settlement and self-government in Essex – the parish – is neatly defined by a historian early in the 20th century: 'Centuries before universal suffrage was ever dreamt of, we were governing ourselves . . . the local community was the only real authority; the parish was the unit of government . . . . Every householder had to serve his year as an administrator of the nation's business . . . he became for the time being an essential part of the national machinery . . . . At the end of his year he went back into the general body of the village community . . .' He was then much wiser about the doings of the parish and its relationship to the county and the country at large. He told his family all he saw and heard, and that was a valuable part of their education.

The parish in the earliest days was what could be described as 'the territorial basis of community service.' The date on which parish government was lawfully defined and introduced is now lost in history, though historians seem to agree that it was some time between the Council of Clermont in 1095 and the Lateran Council of 1179. Parish government was overtaken by the vast increase in population and the formation of large urban areas of residence, business and manufacture. K B Smellie, in his history of local government, shows how this was catered for: 'Between the parish and the King there was a system of county government and in each County the representatives of the King were never allowed to become the independent heads of petty kingdoms . . . certain small towns received special privileges from the King which, in effect, meant that they were excluded from the supervision of the County authorities – those special towns were the Boroughs.'

In later times, and especially during periods of agricultural depression, more and more people were attracted to the opportunities of steady work in the growing urban areas, particularly east and north east of London. The old parishes had to be divided and subdivided to provide the basic services to the poor, the aged and the infirm. Take, for example, the parish of Barking, already shown in Pigot's *County Directory* of 1839 as divided into four wards known as Town, Chadwell, Ilford and Ripple with a total population of 8,000 souls. 'The welfare of the place mainly depends upon its fishery, which employs upwards of twelve hundred men and boys, on board vessels from forty to sixty tons . . . a considerable number of the inhabitants are also engaged in the cultivation of potatoes and other vegetables for the supply of the metropolis.'

By the time the last *County Directory* was published in 1937 both these industries were totally obsolete. Wharves, warehouses and factories had increased and the population in 1931, when Barking achieved the status of a Borough in its own right, was no less than 51,270. Currently, as a new, enlarged London Borough taking in the neighbouring Borough of Dagenham, the population is in the order of 180,000, and industries range from manufacture of cars and production of electricity to industries based on chemicals, paints, timber, rubber and medicines.

In contrast to this expansion, let us look at a country parish – Great Bardfield, in the centre of agricultural Essex. In 1831 it had a population of a thousand and was described as '. . . once a market town, but at present hardly recognizable as such.' By 1937 that population had dwindled to 795. Agricultural inventions, harnessed to the internal combustion engine, were already reducing the manual labour needed on the farm, and competition from foreign food suppliers through advances in canning and refrigeration were affecting the local farming industry.

The universality of personal motor transport today allows anyone with sufficient money to buy a house in a charming village and travel to work in a distant town. Many Essex villages are now dormitories for commuters to London and to the towns in the county – Chelmsford, Colchester, Brentwood, Southend, Stansted and so on.

Even in the earliest days, agriculture was not the only or even the main industry in some places. We have seen how Barking's importance grew from fishing, and there were other places which relied on the sea for their livelihood. Some, like Leigh, were not only busy ports but had their own oyster beds and dredged the estuarine shallows for the shellfish which were the 'beef' in the diet of coastal villagers. Old Walden gained the 'Saffron' prefix from its cultivation of the saffron crocus, so useful in baking and in dyeing. But however the people of Essex earn their living today, the county is now home to a population estimated at more than two and a half million.

2

᷄ EARLIEST ESSEX PEOPLE

T he date of the appearance of Early Man in Essex can be ascertained only in the vaguest terms. When Britain was still joined to the continent there may have been people who pushed across what we now call Europe towards the west of the landmass. Some of those pioneers settled along the river valleys of today's Essex, where the climate was encouraging and the supply of water plentiful.

Evidence of the settlement of these early Palaeolithic people in Essex is scanty but definite. Worked flints and flakes dated from around 13,000 BC have been found in the Colne valley and at Shoeburyness. One of the reports on recent work issued by the Council for British Archaeology, No 34: *Archaeology in Essex*, gives the best account of evidence supporting the settlement of ancient man in this county. It puts forward the theory that, as sea level in palaeolithic times would have been 100 feet or so below the present level, the camping sites of these first settlers now lie under deep, inaccessible sediment. They were followed, around 8,500 BC by Mesolithic (Middle Stone Age) immigrants during a period lasting to around 2,500 BC, the second stage in the story of Essex man as a hunter and food-gatherer when the climate was warm, moist and favourable to their way of life.

The flat, tundra-like countryside was slowly being clothed in pine and birch trees with animals migrating through them in their seasonal travelling – animals which to man the hunter were the embodiment of his vital food, clothing and bone for implements. The cleverly chipped flint points and cutters used in exploiting the creatures he killed have been found at Widford near Chelmsford, near Manningtree and on the coast at Stone Point north of the Naze, at the beginning of the Walton Channel. An antler found near Waltham Holy Cross on the western boundary of the county shows signs of its adaptation as a tool by Mesolithic man. These early Essex ancestors had also mastered the technique of making pottery.

A large number of flint implements have been recovered recently from sand and gravel pits at White Colne, Dawes Heath, Thundersley and in the region of Elsenham Cross. These, together with similar finds from the Cloister site at Waltham Abbey and a field at Great Baddow, are thought by experts to have been used by these early Mesolithic people. The White Colne site included depressions in the ground which it is thought were pits dug more than 5,000 years ago to make subsurface dwellings for survival through the winter. By the close of this period the scattered communities, living by hunting animals and gathering the fruits of the forest and the grain of the clearings, were hearing from new immigrants tales of life in the more ancient eastern civilisation.

The new wave of settlers, the Neolithic (New Stone Age) people were set on new paths by these influences; they changed from chance food-gathering to purposeful food production, founded hill camps, made religious buildings and earthworks and learned the craft of moulding tools, weapons and utensils in bronze. Essex had no stone from which a Stonehenge could be erected but it has been proved by recent archaeological excavation that on the slope of the rise from the river Chelmer to Springfield a timber 'henge' had been erected at the end of a long 'cursus' – land enclosed by two high banks and their associated ditches running parallel over hundreds of yards. The effort required of such primitive people to carry out this work must have been enormous, but expert J D Hedges says, 'They are perhaps the least understood of all prehistoric earthworks and are thought to be unique to Britain. Along with causewayed enclosures and henges they provide insights into social organisation and motivation not witnessed prior to the Neolithic age.' Other possible examples yet to be investigated are situated at Lawford, Great Holland, Wormingford, Little Horkesley, and Dedham.

The continuation of man's successful development is shown in further finds in the Colne Valley and Wicken Bonhunt and in two important collections of 'microliths' – small flakes of flint fashioned to fit on wood, bone or horn as tools or weapons – gathered from the area of Walton-on-the-Naze and from Hullbridge on the Crouch. These tools have been dated by experts to around 5,000 BC and there are enough of them to suggest that the Walton site was a manufacturing area for tools and weapons which were traded far inland.

At Hullbridge, worked flints have been recovered which ante-date the Bronze Age pottery also found on the north bank of the Crouch. It is amazing to think that Stone Age people could use these flint tools to such good effect that they could cut down a large tree, hollow out its trunk and thus fashion a 'dug-out' boat some ten feet long and three to four feet wide in which they put to sea to dredge up oysters, cockles and other shellfish. Walton has yielded just such a dug-out, and a paddle, dated to around 4,000 years ago, was found in the marshy mud off Lion Point above Walton in 1936.

Over the period of some 2,000 years down to 2,000 BC, these New Stone Age people in our county showed their resilience and their resourcefulness. They cleared the forest for their settlements, they reared animals instead of hunting and they grew cereals from gathered grain, storing the harvest to see them through the winter. They ground it to flour with 'querns' – stone handmills, and their ingenuity in flintknapping produced a very wide range of specialist tools to make daily living easier. Yet for all this evidence of their artefacts there are very few clues to fill out the wider picture of their social organisation, and their religious rituals. There is also a paucity of evidence on or under the ground of their simple homes, though sites have been identified from their pottery, tools and grinding stones. Such sites have been found in general distribution across the county, from Thurrock and Mucking to Danbury, Rivenhall, Lawford and, away to the northwest, Newport. Other sites quoted by the CBA report as producing examples of high quality Neolithic flints and pottery have been found along the coast from the mouth of the Blackwater to that of the Stour. The sea, in geological changes, had flooded such settlements, deposited its mud and slime and then, after centuries, had retreated to leave these relics of our Essex ancestors locked in a layer of ocean-bed detritus.

As the North Sea was being formed and England finally became separated from the continent, Essex received a large number of immigrants and traders who dared to brave the channel in their primitive boats. The Beaker Folk, so-called from the beaker-shaped pottery decorated with patterns in horizontal bands found in their graves, made the journey in large numbers. People living on the Beechenlea estate in Chelmsford probably do not realise that Beaker folk had made their homes there some 4,000 years before that. These people were the forerunners of the Early Bronze Age, beginning around 2,000 BC. It lasted about 300 years, giving way over a period of 1,000 years to the Middle and then the Late Bronze Age with its obvious improvements in arts and crafts, based on the techniques of the civilisations established in the Mediterranean region. In Essex the Bronze Age has been reckoned to have started in the period 1,200–1,400 BC, continuing on down to 500 BC. In those scattered settlements by lakes and rivers, where the all-pervading forest gave an air of brooding mystery and a religion of spirits of the woods, of water and of fertility, decorative art, art for the sake of it, was born. All the museums in the county have pieces of pottery made from local clay, items of practical utility, yet patiently adorned with pricked and incised decoration. The implements made in bronze by these people often imitated those stone tools which man had laboured so long to perfect; but bronze workers soon found that a spearhead lashed to a shaft was not nearly as efficient as one moulded in one piece with a socket into which the shaft could be forced. So man used his reason to master his materials and as the Age progressed the bronze mouldings became more technically perfect, at the same time carrying a finish and sometimes decoration which was quite superlative.

Here in Essex the hoards of the bronzesmiths give unassailable evidence of their time and place in history. The smith had routes by which he travelled between the settlements, offering his services, selling new tools and weapons and replacing or restoring old ones. His material was heavy, so he

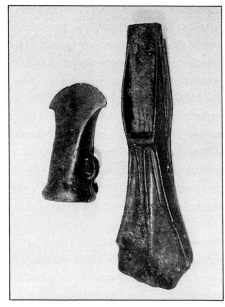

A Bronze Age socketed axe (left) and palstave (right), one of the many examples found in Essex. The palstave was an axe or 'celt', moulded in bronze to fit into a split pole. The new medium enabled the bronze workers to develop their implements beyond the simple stone age spearhead lashed to a shaft.

made caches of it, to be picked up as he came that way again in the next season. We can see this from the discovery of just such a hoard at Hatfield Broad Oak in 1893, which included not only the metals to be fused (copper and tin), but also the earthenware pot in which it had been buried. That hoard is now in the Colchester and Essex Museum. A hoard from High Roding is in the British Museum and another, from Romford, can be seen in the Saffron Walden Museum. Other hoards have been found at Baddow, Danbury, Elmdon, Wendons Ambo, Fyfield, Thundersley and Grays, showing that Essex was more settled in Bronze Age times than is realised by most people today. Spears, daggers, swords and axes from all over Essex can be seen in large numbers in national and local museums.

Because Essex was the first landfall across the sea from France and the Low Countries, waves of immigrants coming across introduced all the news and ideas of that burgeoning civilisation, while further to the west of England old ways, old beliefs and more primitive crafts lingered on. So while Essex folk embraced the new civilisation based on the use of iron, people in the west were still painfully moulding their bronze tools. During this Iron Age from, say, 550 BC to the coming of the Romans in

21

AD 43, the inhabitants of Essex were coalescing into organised groups; tribes we might call them, which had considerable intercourse and trade with Europe, the outposts of the Roman Empire and with Rome itself. In fact the Latin names of these tribes are still used: the Trinovantes occupied eastern Essex, based on their fort Camulodunum at Colchester; the Catuvellauni ruled the west from their fort at Verulamium (St Albans); the Iceni to the north had their capital at Caistor, which the Romans called Venta Icenorum. South of Essex, across the Thames, the Canti tribe were settling down in what is now called Kent.

We cannot leave the Iron Age without mentioning a very special trade in Essex which left marks on the landscape that are still evident today. People who do not really know Essex say it is flat. How surprised they must be when they open their map and find 'Red Hills' shown right on the coast – which could not be flatter! The fact is that they are not very big hills, they are just mounds – man-made mounds more than 2,500 years old. Some of them are 30 acres in extent, even though they rise no more than five feet above the original soil. I say 'original' because these mounds are not soil dug out and heaped up by Iron Age man; they are the waste product he left behind. It is not as if there are just a couple of these wide-spreading low Red Hills; despite the fact that

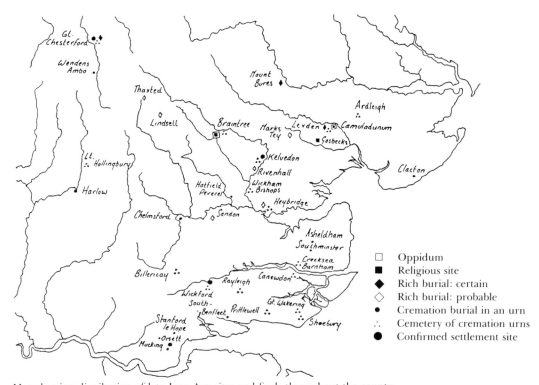

Map showing distribution of late Iron Age sites and finds throughout the county.

22

many of them have been ploughed down or washed away by the sea, there are still up to 200 left all along the coast from Burnham to Clacton.

The old history books only mentioned them as a complete mystery. Modern archaeology tells us the reason for the Red Hills was salt. Ancient man needed salt. He collected it on the sea shore, dried out from tidal pools by the summer sun. He saw that sea water, heated up, would boil away and leave its salt behind. That salt, the gold of the Iron Age, could be traded far inland for other vital necessities like tools, weapons and hides. So he made big, wide, shallow pans of thick, crude pottery, put them as near the tide as he could, filled them with sea water, then lit a fire beneath them, using the brush and timber he could gather on the foreshore. When the water boiled away he scraped up the salt, added it to a growing store, then set off inland with it to trade.

Sometimes the pans broke; their pieces were simply left lying in the growing pile of ashes. The amount of such detritus accumulating over a hundred years of salt production defies the imagination. Since Roman pottery has been found in these piles of reddish burnt soil and ashes, there is proof that the Essex salt industry continued on into Christian times and that is why the Red Hills reached such enormous proportions. Many of them were dug out and scattered over farmers' fields from the 18th century onwards when the value of wood ash as a fertilizer became appreciated.

The archaeologist Paul Drury, writing in 1980, tells us: '125 early and middle Iron Age sites are known in the county, mostly casual finds of pottery in gravel or brickearth pits.' He suggests that the more field systems of pre-Roman origin are discovered, the more one must accept that the Iron Age farmers had considerably altered the landscape by the time the Romans marched in, in AD 43. And, of course, these farmers went on sowing crops and rearing animals from which the Romans demanded their tribute. From the eighth to the seventh century BC the Bronze Age settlers and craftsmen merged with the men mastering the new technology of working in iron. Iron, so strong and so malleable under heat, superseded bronze. Further developments with the use of iron, including fittings for the potter's wheel, had been introduced by the time Julius Caesar appeared on the scene around 55 BC.

Hill forts were a characteristic of settlement in the Iron Age as a whole and surprisingly, considering its general lack of high hills, Essex is not deficient in them. They were constructed on the edge of necks of higher land, with a good view on three sides where possible. Ambresbury Banks in Epping Forest is the best-known example. Gryme's Dyke is a 3½ mile-long rampart built as a western defence for the great tribal

The Bronze Age Dagenham Idol, a figure carved in wood, discovered near the Ford factory at Dagenham. Close by was found a skeleton of a deer – a sacrifice, it is thought, to this carved image of a god of fertility.

capital of Camulodunum. Epping Forest contains another fort in the shape of Loughton Camp. From its southern side it was possible to see clear across the Thames to Kent. The strange Repell or Paille ditches at Saffron Walden date from this time, though the skeletons found on the site are from a later, Saxon cemetery. The camp on the hill overlooking Audley End is another landmark, and so is Wallbury Camp at Great Hallingbury, where the double ramparts enclose no less than 35 acres. This is one of the later earthworks, without the complicated series of ditches which protected a serpentine entrance. Apparently this was a place designed for the quick assembly and rapid deployment of a body of fighting men. Other sites identified as Iron Age fortifications are at Danbury, Asheldham, Witham and South Weald.

One site which yielded invaluable information about our Iron Age ancestors is Little Waltham. Though a find of funerary pottery was found quite crushed, flattened by its heavy blanket of silt, it has been restored to its former beauty and can be seen in the Chelmsford and Essex Museum, along with a complete report of all the finds associated with the clan which built its round huts in the vale of the Chelmer where the Little Waltham bypass now speeds the modern traffic on its way. Another motoring connection is made at Dagenham, for there, not far from the vast complex of the Ford factory, in the marsh right by the river, was found the 'Dagenham Idol'. Nearby the skeleton of a deer was found, and this, it has been postulated, could have been a sacrifice to win the favour of this god of fertility.

It may well be that while a craftsman was carving the Dagenham Idol, there were people of the tribe at Saffron Walden carving out a maze, by the tread of their feet, for similar religious purposes. The Maze, at the eastern end of the Common, abutting Chater's Hill, is claimed to be the best earthen maze still surviving in England. Such mazes have always been associated with the fertility rites of these ancient peoples. Even down to the 18th century, according to a record of the time, the Maze was the scene of fun and games for the boys and girls of the town. A girl would stand in the centre of the Maze while a boy tried to reach her, following the windings of the way worn in the turf, without leaving the path or falling over.

The Maze covers a circle of about 100 feet in diameter with concentric circles cut in the turf around a centrepiece of raised earth. At each corner there is also a smaller platform, and the whole maze is enclosed by a low bank. Aerial photography shows a dark circular patch just to the west of the present maze which is thought to have been the first 'stamping ground' of a prehistoric tribe which trod these paths in a dance they hoped would placate and bring the blessings of a great god of fertility. Two points for walkers of today – you are supposed to start on the north side, and you walk in the ditch, not on the raised turf. As we follow in their footsteps we cannot appreciate the intensity of their frenzied dancing in the hope that their gods would cause their crops to flourish in the coming year; for if their crudely cultivated corn failed, they faced starvation.

It was the immigration of the Belgae people from the lowlands into Kent around 75 BC that profoundly influenced the development of Essex as a whole. Within 20 years they had spread north across the Thames, and by 50 BC the Belgae were a force to be reckoned with – gradually absorbing the smaller native tribes. They brought with them the invention of the wheeled plough – coulters for such a plough were excavated at Great Chesterford, an old native township later fortified and completely walled by the Romans.

At this time the leader of the Catevellauni was Cunobelin. He had taken over northern Essex and by the first half of the first century AD had built up his capital at Camulodunum into a great commercial centre. The reign of Cunobelin is considered as the beginning of the Romanisation of Britain – as much by trade as by invasion.

3

ROMAN ESSEX

T here is no doubt that Essex was the centre of the stage in the great drama of the Roman conquest of Britain in AD 43. One reason for the invasion was the acquisition of further territory through armed superiority. The Romans had overcome the larger country of the Gauls but after Julius Caesar landed in Kent in 54 BC, he could not sustain a presence. A hundred years later Emperor Claudius saw that much personal prestige could be gained from a successful invasion and a triumphal procession through Rome with slaves and booty. Some Roman traders were already settled in Essex. They, the members of the Emperor's entourage and the officers of his army were all keen to benefit from a share in the spoils. Another reason for the invasion at this time was that Cunobelin had just died. He was of the line and tribe of Cassivellaunus, and he had conquered the Trinovantes to rule at Camulodunum (Colchester) as well as at Verulamium (St Albans), and possibly had overcome the northern tribe of the Iceni. He has been called the first British King. Suetonius, the contemporary Roman biographer described him as 'Rex Britannorum'.

Cunobelin had trouble with his son Adminius, finally expelling him from Britain and when he died he left his kingdom to his other two sons. Adminius meanwhile had sought the help of Emperor Caligula, who himself died in AD 41. Thus was set in motion the invasion under Aulus Plautius in AD 43 when Emperor Claudius was in power. It was a glorious victory. As Camulodunum was the capital of such a large area and the most important town in Britain at that time, the Romans came in on the Kent coast, crossed the Thames and headed for it with the utmost speed. What the Romans found was a big, busy town at the head of the Colne on a promontory of rising ground which was a 100 ft high plateau aligned east–west, protected on the north by the river Colne, on the south by its tributary the Roman River, with marshes on the south and east and woodland on the north and west. Three and a half miles of earthworks had been built across the neck of this promontory as further protection, marked on today's maps as 'Gryme's Dyke'. This settlement had been trading with Rome for 50 years already, so the coming of the

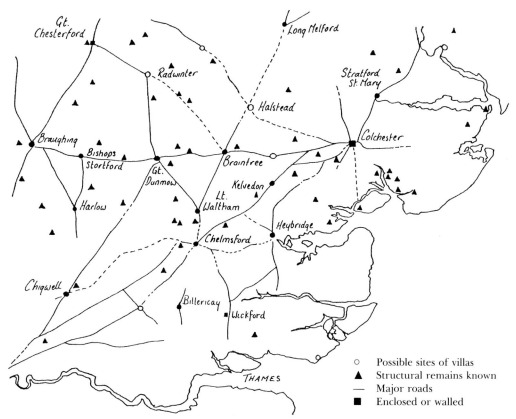

○	Possible sites of villas
▲	Structural remains known
—	Major roads
■	Enclosed or walled

Map showing the Roman system of roads in Essex, with the position of structural remains and possible sites of Roman villas.

soldiers was more in the nature of an enforced takeover than a laying-waste. Emperor Claudius was determined to introduce to the tribes of Essex and beyond the civilised, systematic way of life as lived in Rome. The sheer power of Roman military and civil government organisation impressed the tribal chiefs and aided pacification. Their prowess in road building allowed speedy movement of troops and the improved transport of exports through Roman merchants.

The site of the first camp set up by the expeditionary force south east of Camulodunum was discovered in 1931, and here it was that, in about AD 50, the Romans set up their new town of Colonia Victricensis – a settlement for discharged soldiers who did not wish to return home. It was utterly destroyed within twelve years during the Boudiccan revolt. Undeterred, the Romans rebuilt the whole town, enclosed its 108 acres in a 3,100 yard long wall and set out the streets on the usual grid plan of right-angled intersections. One famous archaeologist, Dr Wheeler, suggests that the great Balkerne Gate in those walls was specially built to celebrate the completion of the long straight roads out of the 'Colonia' to London and St Albans. Others have taken its history further by referring to the name 'Balkerne' as meaning that this gate was blocked up to 'balk' attempts by raiding Danes or Saxons to enter the town from that direction. The importance of the Colchester of those days is indicated by the great temple of Claudius, remains of which are to be seen to this day in the cellars of the Castle. It demonstrated the town's status as the religious centre of the whole province. Yet for some unknown reason the town did not grow and soon London had surpassed it in trade and administrative importance. At least four other places in Roman Britain soon ranked above the old British capital and Colchester gradually became a small country town with a modest trade with the continent.

With the capital in their hands, the Romans set about appeasement and pacification. They developed points of entry for supplies at Fingringhoe Wick, serving Colchester and the northern area, and at Heybridge, already a trading port, serving central Essex and the garrison at Chelmsford. It is possible that Bradwell-on-Sea, where later a shore-fort was built, had been a Roman naval base.

It is hard to believe from the peaceful, rural view of Great Chesterford today that it was once a major military fortress covering 30 acres, built by the Romans after the Boudiccan uprising. There is no sign of a single stone on the surface and much of the subsoil which would have contained remains has been carried away in gravel extraction. It would seem that it controlled the several routes leading north to the Icknield Way. The Romans pacified the natives by improving their smaller towns, which attracted people from the surrounding countryside with their shops, stalls and crafts, providing for the everyday needs of the inhabitants. Examples have been found at Heybridge, Kelvedon and Chelmsford. Details of this type of Romanised smaller town can be gathered from reports by archaeologists like Drury and Rodwell, including the CBA Research Report No 34 of 1980. Cropmark evidence in aerial surveys shows that Iron Age and subsequent Roman settlement was extensive on the lighter soils north of the Thames and on the vales of the Colne, the Blackwater and the Stour. Roman occupation made no great change in the Essex countryside. Small Iron Age settlements became villages or small towns, usually at road junctions or river crossings. Gradually the larger Roman 'villas' were built in selected spots from which their rich and influential owners could commute to centres of government administration, business and trade.

It had been thought that the great invasion left little trace of its passage through Essex because military occupation and government was so brief, but recent excavations have brought more evidence to light. Marching camps were at river crossings to water man and beast of burden, and to allow the column to catch up. One such stopping place would have been at Chelmsford by the rivers Can and Chelmer, roughly halfway between the Thames and the great capital at Colchester. A ditch was discovered which bore the marks of the stakes which made a crude but effective palisade against surprise attack. That camp developed into a trading centre, winning over the local tribe by peaceful means, but a military presence is thought to have remained for some 40 years. Though the Trinovantes had long been allies of Rome, no chances were taken. The Romans sited small forts along the high road they had soon engineered. One is known to have existed at Kelvedon and it is thought that there were others at Braintree and Great Dunmow.

At Orsett an enclosure with three surrounding ditches suggests such a fort, but no military finds have come to light. Wickford, Hadleigh and West Tilbury have also produced evidence of defensive earthworks. Durolitum, a fortified settlement mentioned by Roman historians, has not yet been identified, though Rodwell places it near Chigwell from external evidence. Tolleshunt D'Arcy, Great Wakering, Marks Tey and Waltham Cross have all yielded items of military significance. As the tribe settled peacefully under Roman rule, these fortified settlements took on urban status. Places like Chelmsford developed as tribal market centres. Its Latin name – 'Caesaromagus' – means, according to some, Caesar's Market.

With today's rapid building developments, more prehistoric and Roman remains have been discovered in Essex in the last 20 years than ever before. Many of them have been covered up again, smashed by great earthmovers or carried away unnoticed in massive lorry-loads of unwanted subsoil. Essex County Council has set up an archaeology department to investigate any reported finds. A good idea of the extent of the Roman occupation of Essex can be gained from a glance through the pages of the volume produced by the *Victoria County History* in 1963 to provide a gazetteer of all the places in Essex where evidence had been found of Roman activity. To take just one place as an example – Great Chesterford. Apart from Colchester it is the only Roman town in Essex known to have been walled all round. Yet, as recently as 1945 a rush job had to be made of archaeological excavation in advance of gravel working which was being allowed to strip the whole site.

Long before then, back in the 18th century, the Roman walls were being pulled down for the valuable building rubble they afforded. Coins were so plentiful all over the area, including those of Cunobelin, that an archaeologist reported they were 'universal all over the ground.' In 1719 Stukeley, the well known antiquarian, said that the landlord of the Crown Inn was selling such coins at 4d a time. It is not surprising that there was so much money about, for one of the buildings of which archaeologists recently found the foundations was a Roman tax office – built around AD 200.

The Romans did not have it all their own way. Archaeologists digging today in Colchester and Chelmsford often come across a layer of burnt material – mute evidence of the day when the Iceni rose in open revolt. The circumstances and the outcome are well described in the introduction to William Cowper's poems published in 1782:

> 'Boadicea, or Boudicca, was the wife of Prasutagus, King of the Iceni, the people who occupied during Roman times the greater part of the country now called East Anglia. On the death of Prasutagus, in AD 60, Boadicea became head of the Iceni. Although a warlike race, the Iceni, as a result of revolts, had been reduced by the Romans to a state of virtual servitude. Taking advantage of the will of Prasutagus, under which the King's property was to be divided between his daughters and the Roman Emperor, the Roman officials claimed the whole. Boadicea was flogged, and her family outrageously treated.
>
> Led by Boadicea, the Iceni, joined by the Trinobantes [sic] of the south, rose in revolt. Colchester was taken by them and even London itself. The Roman Governor, who was away in Anglesey, returned to meet the Iceni. Before the battle, which ended in defeat for the Iceni, Boadicea roused her army by driving with her daughters through the lines of her warriors, reminding them of all the insults she had suffered. Boadicea ended her life by poison and the Roman power became supreme in Eastern England.'

There is no doubt that the fury of Boudicca's tribesmen left complete devastation in their wake as they laid waste to Colchester, burned much of Chelmsford and then attempted to set light to London. The site of the last battle against the Romans, when her troops were routed, has never been positively identified, though legend has it that it was at Ambresbury Banks in Epping Forest.

In all the burning and the looting, the killing and the maiming, there is one strange tale of how a Roman soldier's tombstone was preserved through the vandalism of Boudicca's men. It is a tombstone to a Roman soldier who died peacefully while serving as a 'corporal' in the First Regiment of the Thracian Cavalry, stationed in the ancient British capital of Camulodunum, or Colchester, as part of the occupation force. Though the stone is broken the inscription on it can be read as distinctly as when it was first put up, around AD 60. It tells us that Corporal Longinus came from Sardica and was the son of Matycus Sdapeze. He had served 15 years with the army, probably came over with the expeditionary force in AD 43, and was 40 when he died. It is a splendid monument: the upper half shows, deeply carved, Longinus in all his glory as a Roman trooper, mounted on his stocky, strong-looking horse, trampling underfoot a cowering British warrior. The stone was vandalised almost as soon as it was put up because, when Boudicca led her troops through Colchester in revolt against the Roman yoke in AD 61, they pushed on through the Roman cemetery, and were incensed to see this monument showing one of their warriors being hacked down in the dust. They smashed the stone down, it was never re-erected and slowly became covered with the detritus of time. It was not found again until 1928 when it was excavated from the Roman cemetery in Beverley Road and transferred to the Colchester and Essex Museum.

The tombstone of Longinus Sdapeze, defaced in Boudicca's assault on Colchester in AD61, and undiscovered until 1928.

When the revolt had been put down the old threads of cultured and civilised life were taken up again in that part of the Roman province of Britain we now call Essex. Some evidence of this can be gathered from other items on view in the Roman collection in that same museum: all kinds of pots and pans, in daily use in the 'Colonia', reflect a well-provided kitchen for the better off, be they Roman or British; oil lamps

The Colchester Vase, of Roman origin, decorated with animals and gladiators and of black Caistor ware, was one of a number of pots found grouped together in a Roman burial site. It is one of Colchester museum's outstanding exhibits.

of superior design and decoration which lit the winter nights, and luxury objects in glass, pottery and precious stones – art for art's sake, and demonstrating the status and the taste of their owners. Of all the spheres of human activity represented in this absorbing collection, the most surprising must be the wide range of aids to beauty which the Roman matron's maids could use to bring their mistress's beauty to perfection. There are bottles and pots which contained the unguents, and the tiny, fragile bronze spoons to extract them; the cosmetics, eye-black and rouge from the long-necked miniature containers; tweezers, pins of bronze and bone – all are there; and in the days when they were in daily use the great Ovid gave advice which has been translated thus:

'Always beware that from your lover's eyes
You keep concealed these toilet mysteries;
Though art assists, yet must that art be hid,
Lest where it would invite it should forbid;
For many things, when done afford delight,
Which yet, in doing, may offend the sight.'

Further evidence of the increasing fraternisation between conquerors and conquered is shown in the Bartlow Hills in the parish of Ashdon, on the northern boundary of Essex, four miles north east of Saffron Walden. Bartlow is the name of the adjoining parish. Angela Green, writing *Ashdon* explains:

'The most spectacular remains of the Roman period in the parish are the Bartlow Hills which lie within the Ashdon parish boundary. There some of the local inhabitants erected the burial mounds or barrows known as the Hills, in which they buried their dead. The Hills stood in two rows near the present road. The four larger, steep-sided mounds must have been conspicuous landmarks, the

32

largest 40 feet high, and made of alternate layers of up to a foot deep of earth and chalk, so that before the grass had taken root, selfsown, on the steep sides the brightness of the white chalk contrasting with the earth must have made the new burial place visible from a considerable distance.'

There were at one time nine 'hills' standing close together, like old-time conical sugar loaves. These were the last resting places of the families of local rulers – people of consequence – who were absorbing many of the habits, customs and beliefs of their Roman overlords. As each person died, over a period of 50 years from the end of the first century AD, their kin arranged opulent funerals where the corpses were burnt on a pyre, the ashes collected, and placed in pottery or glass urns. A chamber was fashioned in the partially built mound and the urn was placed within it, accompanied by some of the deceased's possessions for use in their after-life, such as a folding chair made of iron and bronze, an iron hanging lamp and a wooden bucket bound with bronze hoops. There is evidence that food and drink had been placed in pottery and glass containers, one brilliantly enamelled in the Roman 'La Tene' style.

These mounds stood up to 45 ft high and measured some 144 ft in diameter at the foot. Two of the smaller ones were ploughed down, one of them in 1586. Three others were levelled under the orders of the landowner, Henry, Viscount Maynard, in 1832. He had them carefully excavated and even called in the famous Michael Faraday, founder of the science of electro-magnetism, to examine and report on the utensils in the chambers. Faraday was also asked to look at the items found when a tunnel was driven to the centre of the largest 'Hill' in 1835. In 1838 and 1840 three more tombs were excavated, yielding bronze utensils and glass vessels. All were added to Lord Maynard's private museum at Easton Lodge, except the enamelled jar, which went to the British Museum. In 1847 Easton Lodge was burned down in a terrible fire and all the museum exhibits were lost. How fortunate it was that the British Museum had been given the prize exhibit! When the line of the railway was excavated in 1865, bisecting these mounds, 15 skeletons were found, proof that after cremation was discontinued as a funerary rite the Romano-British people went on to bury their dead in this place revered by their ancestors.

Evidence of a more humble state of Romano-British life was found recently in a rubbish pit, four ft below ground level, sliced through by the blade of a bulldozer preparing the ground on the Widford Industrial estate, south west of Chelmsford. From the bits and pieces thrown into that rubbish pit by a Romano-British family some 1,800 years ago it can be deduced that the walls of their homestead were wattle and daub and the roof probably thatched. A hard tramped layer of clay over pebbles found nearby was the original floor. The farmer cultivated the land he had cleared from the forest down to the bank of the river Wid, growing cereals and keeping a few sheep and goats as well as the pigs which he turned loose in the forest to grub for acorns and roots.

The most evident reminder of the Roman presence in Essex must be those long, straight roads whose ruler-like directness can be appreciated more on the map or from the air than on the ground. There had been tracks tramped through forests from clearing to clearing by the British tribes, who had already developed trade routes for salt from the coast and the products of the Bronze and Iron Ages, but the Romans took them over where necessary and transformed them into wide roads based on proper engineering principles. They were already skilled in making roads throughout Europe to supply the garrisons of their vast empire, so, having captured the great British capital of Camulodunum, for use as their headquarters, they improved all the existing tracks which radiated from it and introduced new roads.

The track from the Thames to the native capital was upgraded into a well-paved road constructed of graded stones, cambered and drained. The old route from Camulodunum to Verulamium was improved in the same way, earning the name of Stane Street (the paved way), from their Saxon successors. The Ordnance Survey's 'Map of Roman Britain' gives the most reliable and complete picture of the Roman road system throughout the county. The old A12 followed the line of the main Roman road from Colchester to London. In its path lay the Romanised settlements of Kelvedon (Canonicum), Caesaromagus (Chelmsford) and Durolitum – unidentified, but thought to be in the region of Romford.

Roads out of the East Gate of Colchester towards the next big town of Caister St Edmunds shared the same way down to East Bridge. When an opportunity arose to cut a section across it archaeologists found '. . . a cambered surface of gravel metalling 12 in thick, laid on 2 ft of clay' (*Victoria County History*). Great Chesterford was at the centre of roads to Braughing in Hertfordshire, and to Cambridge as a continuation to the north. Its popular name, the Icknield Way, has been traced in written records as far back as 1208, when it is shown as Ykenild. A later mention, in 1387, of the Ikening Way may refer to the ancient track which ran through the land of the Iceni. Another road ran south east to Thaxted and Great Easton, and possibly, on to Great Dunmow. From Dunmow another road still runs straight to Aythorpe Roding. Putting a straight edge on a modern map, one can see a continuation of this important road south west all the way through the county to the large

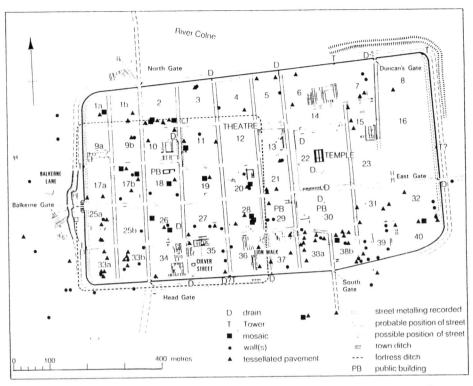

Roman Colchester around AD300 showing the position of the town wall and the fortress defences.

Roman settlement just east of the river Roding and the M11 in the parish of Chigwell. The first part, from Dunmow, is known by oral tradition as the Suffolk Way, but no continuation in that direction north east of Dunmow has been found.

Another very obvious Roman road is that from Chelmsford to Braintree, on up to Gosfield and Gestingthorpe, and so into Suffolk. The puzzle of the Roman network of roads has interested people from as early as the 18th century. Nathaniel Salmon, writing the *New Survey of England* in 1728, propounded a way from Colchester to Cambridge without touching Great Chesterford but excavations have not yet yielded evidence to support it. The same lack of success has attended efforts to delineate a road from Colchester to Mersea Island. This is disappointing because the Island has yielded abundant evidence of a Roman settlement. It was a place already well peopled when the Romans came. The many Red Hills are proof of that. Roman occupation in settled post-Boudiccan days is illustrated by the floor of a fine Roman house found lying beneath the churchyard and the Hall at West Mersea. Excavations in 1730 and 1956 in the garden and the adjoining burial ground allowed

35

archaeologists to estimate that the complete and very beautiful mosaic floor measures 21 ft 6 in by 18 ft. Related finds around the Hall prove that this Roman villa was of huge proportions.

The striking find on this island was made about 200 yards east of that Roman villa. It is a Romano-British wheel tomb, so described because of its walls: the 'spokes' radiating out from a central chamber, the 'hub' meeting a circular perimeter wall, the 'rim' three ft thick and 65 ft in circumference. In the central chamber the ashes of a wealthy Romano-British inhabitant were placed in an urn of coloured glass. The urn was not found, but there was one in a simpler tomb found a foot deep just a few yards to the east. The late M R Hull explains the reason for this grand demonstration of status in the *Victoria County History*: 'The monumental Roman tomb based upon the tumulus appealed to native aristocrats or dynasts, among whom the tumulus was still *par excellence* the form of a princely grave, and it came naturally to wealthy . . . Britons to be buried according to the old fashion, in the new manner.'

Nearer the middle of the Island is Barrow Hill Farm. Its name commemorates the great Roman tumulus still standing here, excavated in 1912. It is 22 ft 6 in high, 16 ft wide at the top and with a diameter at the base of 110 ft. The actual chamber, in which the cremated remains of some local notable were found, measures only 18 in square and 21½ in high. The ashes were in a glass urn within a leaden casket.

As the Roman empire crumbled through the infighting of warring factions and the attacks of the 'barbarians' on its borders, the legions in outposts like Essex were first left to fend for themselves, and later, recalled to the desperate battles in their homeland. The question might be asked, 'What have Essex people inherited from the Romans in terms of ways of life, art, language, literature, customs and crafts?' One answer comes from Francis Haverfield, recognized authority on this period: 'From the Romans who once ruled Britain we Britons have inherited practically nothing.' Perhaps the greatest beneficiaries of the Roman occupation of Essex are the archaeologists – they are delving still.

4

SAXON INVASION AND COLONISATION

Once the 'classis Britannica' – the Roman North Sea fleet – had been withdrawn, the door to Britain was well and truly open to the raiding and settling Saxons – the seafarers from the lands fed by rivers like the Rhine, the Ems and the Weser. They quickly settled the seaward areas of Essex, Suffolk, Norfolk and Kent and moved on westward to places that the Romans had not penetrated. They were looters, who destroyed and burned rather than integrated and settled. But when the warriors had gone, families, the true settlers, came behind them. The impetus of invasion slowed as it flowed westward. The west country and Wales fought off the Saxons to maintain a pastoral way of life which even the mighty Romans had been unable to change.

The endless flow of the new race could not be resisted. By AD 603 the Anglo-Saxons had colonised the country and England, expanded into Britain by their conquests, was now their homeland. They were true settlers – they worked together and for each other: great craftsmen, farmers, husbandmen, loyal to their clan, implacable to their enemies.

In King Alfred, only 21 when he led his 'rustic levies' against the Danes at Ashdown in AD 871, the English nation found its saviour. By his introduction of a navy and the reorganisation of the army this great King threw back the Danish hosts, fortified key 'burghs' or towns and, at the end of his reign, routed the Viking Grand Army. Thus the 'English-ness of England' was preserved. Alfred died around AD 899, worn out by his efforts in serving his country. 'More than any other man,' says Arthur Bryant, 'he was the first maker of England.'

'The transition from Roman Britain to Saxon England has traditionally been seen as one of the more vivid episodes in history, and Essex lies prominently in the middle of the southeastern zone of the primary settlement', says Warwick Rodwell, archaeologist, adding that there is no historical evidence available to lighten the darkness of the period, though recent excavations have shown that some Roman presence lingered well into the fifth century. The fact that the Romans built such large and solid forts as the one at Bradwell shows that Saxon raiding parties were already eyeing the green and pleasant land which offered chances of settlement. Certainly the immigration of Germanic tribes into Essex during the 5th and 6th centuries was not nearly as extensive as that into neighbouring coastal counties. Those forts, the impressive and impregnable walled capital of Camulodunum and minor defended places as at Chelmsford and Great Chesterford, may have continued to act as a temporary deterrent to the less sophisticated Saxons.

For these and other geographical reasons Essex cannot be said to be anything like the starting point of Saxon immigration, so it is very rare indeed that archaeological finds of the first, pagan period of Saxon settlement are found here. Few burials of early Saxons have been found. It would appear that bodies were buried rather than cremated and to date no urn containing calcined human remains has been found in Essex. Signs of early Saxon settlers have been found at widely separated sites, but there may be many more sites as yet unidentified.

The great leap forward in the knowledge of Saxon life in Essex came over the ten years from 1968, following observation from the air of crop marks. In the Mucking area it yielded evidence of occupation by families from neolithic times, until the Saxons left the marks in the ground of their sunken huts, two cemeteries and, on the site of one hut, an almost complete pot, lying abandoned on the floor. Its form and decoration indicated that this was the start of the new Saxon period.

At Rivenhall the Roman buildings of stone were taken over by Anglo-Saxons who lived there as the Romans did, farming a small estate. When those stone buildings gradually fell into ruin somewhere around the 6th century, the Saxons replaced them with the timber buildings of which they were master craftsmen. It is possible that such an estate simply evolved in this way until mentioned at last in the Domesday Book.

The gradual merging of Saxon with Romano-British appeared to continue with very little hostility. In many a cemetery opened up by archaeologists the graves run on from Roman to early Saxon without a visible break; Great Chesterford and Kelvedon both show this steady change of occupants of their settlements. One elaborate Roman burial in the latter place reflected in its construction the Saxon custom of a chamber grave in a timber mausoleum. Anglo-Saxon cemeteries in Colchester, Great Chesterford, Saffron Walden and Wicken Bonhunt show evidence of the new race of British people living and dying. At least 24 other sites show signs of Saxon settlement.

There is a most unusual story of the discovery of treasures from a Saxon grave at Broomfield. In about 1888, farmer David Christy's land in Broomfield was being developed. Christy had ordered some of his men to go into a field behind Clobbs Row, a short street of workers' cottages built at right angles to Broomfield Road, to dig out a load of gravel from the large pit already opened up there. The gravel was being quarried about seven feet below the surface of the field. In digging it out by hand the men came across pieces of a broken, corroded sword, a spear, a knife and other small, not easily identifiable items.

The men, uneducated in ancient history and archaeology, and with no time to stand and stare, took the gravel and left the 'junk' as they found it, still half buried in the gravel. Mr Christy had no need for more gravel from that pit for another six years. Then the labourers who went down in the pit realised it was a grave which had been broken into previously. The remnants of the former digging were still there. They were collected and, under Mr Christy's direction the rest of the grave goods were carefully excavated. They included parts of the decoration of the sword, gold studs set with precious stones. The grave was clearly defined by a black line in the gravel, indicating slow, sooty combustion. Within it a further collection of objects included a bronze pan containing two glass, and two turned wooden cups with rims of gilt bronze. Two wooden buckets were set in the bottom of the grave and in one corner was a two-gallon iron cauldron. No trace of a body was found, but there was evidence in an ashy deposit that a body in a strong wooden coffin had been set alight on interment and slowly smouldered away. Comparison with similar burials in other parts of southern England shows this to have been the grave of an important local Saxon chief of around AD 600. The remains were finally deposited in the British Museum.

In talking of death and burial we are trying to understand, through the only surviving evidence, something of the life and times of the people of the 'shire' of Essex, who organised its local government for the next 1,000 years. F M Stenton, historian of Anglo-Saxon England, says: 'On passing from Anglian into Saxon territory, from East Anglia into Essex, the obscurity deepens. No East Saxon king was of more than local importance; and although an early Saxon occupation of Essex is proved by place-names of a primitive type, no other part of south-eastern England has yielded so little archaeological evidence of its condition in the heathen age.' For him, the chief interest of Saxon Essex lay in the genealogy of the royal house where, like other Saxon kingships, there was a determined attempt to keep a link with the ancestral line in an alliterative naming of successors to the throne. Thus the crown in Essex passed from Sledda to Seaxa, Sigefrith, Selefrith, Sigebald, Sigeberht, Selered, Sigeric and so to Sigered, the last of the line. These names have a further meaning for us in that they carry the root of the two names 'Gesceg Seaxneting', referring to a god still worshipped by the Saxons in their continental homeland down to the 8th century. It would appear that these kings took London as their capital, with Middlesex as a province of their kingdom, but even London has failed to produce evidence of its 6th century past.

The way in which these Saxon immigrants came to settle in Essex in family tribes is illustrated in many of the place-names of present towns and villages. We only have room for a few examples. There were once nine villages with the Roothing or Roding suffix from Abbess Roothing to White Roothing. This whole district was settled by a tribe which probably came in en masse to clear spaces in the forest all along the river which got its name, Roding, from these settlements of the 'ing' or tribe, led by Hrotha.

There is a little chapter of history in the name of the charming village of Ingatestone. Saxon settlers came across a meadow by a river which seemed a good place to put down roots. It was a location easily recognised from the huge boulder left there in prehistory as the glaciers retreated. It may have marked a junction of tracks of the salt trails, before the Romans came. The little settlement prospered, and came to need an identity as immigrants passed through. They called it, 'The place where the folk have settled by the great stone' – in other words, the 'ing' at the stone, which soon became shortened to Ingatestone. Other names reflected the conditions encountered in settling. For example Rayleigh, says Dr Reaney, the place-names expert, simply means 'Wild she-goat clearing', illustrating as clearly as a camera what leapt out of the wood when the pioneers began their first land clearance. Gryme's Dyke, that defensive earthwork so laboriously raised by Iron Age people on the landward side of Camulodunum, was seen by the Saxons as the work of the devil, Grim, as they called him, for they could not envisage men before them altering the landscape on such a vast scale.

Althorne is Saxon for 'burnt thorn bush', and one can imagine how those settlers cursed the thorns through which they forced their way before burning off the whole area to make room for their huts, animals and patches of cereals. Writtle reflects one of the happiest experiences in looking for a place to settle. Pushing past Chelmsford, with its ruinous Roman buildings, they came to the banks of the Wid and found it an ideal place for settlement. They called the river Writtoloburna, 'the babbling, purling stream' and named their village after it. Tolleshunt villages grew up because of the essential spring of water flowing there. Toll was the leader of the tribe, 'hunt' or 'funt' was their name for a spring. Some places got their names from their size. Coggeshall was Cocc's nook, and Cicca had his 'nook' in the Chignalls where Chignall

Smealey had the addition to show it was a 'smooth clearing'.

The still powerful Roman army had remained in England and in Essex until the early years of the 5th century, with a strong element under the command of the Count of the Saxon Shore attempting to discourage invaders. But as central authority from Rome waned and the army of occupation elected its own emperor their power was diminished, Saxons broke through the beleaguered defences of the south and east of England. In AD 410 Honorius, the emperor facing the sack of Rome by the Goths, sent a message to the cities of Britain telling them that henceforward they would be responsible for their own defence. There must have been a long period between the evacuation of the Roman army and the emergence of law and order as provided by the Saxons on a regional basis. It has been suggested that the earliest such organisation may have been at Mucking, where men from the well-established settlement were recruited to man boats to fend off further waves of invaders. This was to no avail: by the end of the 6th century two thirds of what was to become England was in the hands of the tribes of local kings who served overlords of much wider districts than the present county.

The future development of Essex had much to do with the growth of the church and the crusading zeal of missionaries. The early conversion of Romans and Ancient British had failed. All the Anglo-Saxon kings were pagan until St Augustine's mission of AD 597. King Aethelbert of Kent, overlord of the whole of the south of England, was converted soon after Augustine's appearance at his court. The King of Essex, as his vassal, was next to make Christianity the accepted religion of his people, with a bishopric set up at London. When Aethelbert died in AD 616 his son and his successor reverted to paganism, as did the sons of Saberht. Kent was soon back in the fold, but Essex had to wait until about AD 653 before the King accepted the message of Christ through Bishop, later Saint, Cedd. Even then the hold of Christianity over the hearts and minds of the Essex people was tenuous. Their king was so frightened by the dreadful plague of AD 664 that he went back to his pagan gods for reassurance. Nevertheless the Church's hold gradually increased. An interesting legend, handed down by word of mouth for centuries shows that Christianity was flourishing.

Shortly after St Cedd came ashore, Osyth, daughter of the King of the East Saxons, who had grown up in the Christian faith, was presented as Prioress of the nunnery her father had founded for her at, or near, the village of Chich. Chich was the Saxon word for a bend – a bend in the creek which runs down to the Colne estuary. This was where the first Saxons settled. Some time before the 8th century a gang of raiding

St Osyth's Priory, built on the site of the nunnery, founded by Osyth, daughter of the King of the East Saxons, who died for her faith at the hands of marauding Vikings.

Vikings came up the creek and landed here. They were heathens who took delight in laying waste the nunnery fields. They jeered at the terrified nuns and tried to make them renounce their belief, but Osyth stepped forward, confronted the cruel chief, rejected his terms and told him to let her nuns go in peace. He was furious at being castigated by a woman and ordered one of his henchmen to behead her on the spot. Osyth died for her faith, and legend has it she bent down, picked up her head and carried it to the nunnery chapel, where she struck the door with her bloodied hand to show that she wished to be buried within. On the spot where she had been beheaded a spring of the purest water gushed forth, and the place is still known as Nun's Wood. Osyth was later canonised, the village growing round the nunnery became first Chich St Osyth and now St Osyth is part of a five-mile stretch of coastline where thousands of people holiday in the numerous chalets and caravans which line it.

Two other religious buildings still stand to show the faith of Saxon Christians. One is St Peter's Chapel, built to Bishop Cedd's order in the gateway of the ruined Roman fort of Othona at Bradwell-juxta-Mare.

The Saxon church of St Peter on the Wall, reputed to be the first church built on Essex soil.

This is said to be the first church built on Essex soil and there is no reason to dispute this. Cedd had it built here on the spot where he landed to bring the revived mission. The historic significance of his little church was not appreciated as the centuries passed. It was used as a navigation guide for seamen, standing as it does right on the shore, then as a barn until, in 1920, its place in Essex history and religion was recognised and it was reconsecrated, to become the focus of an annual pilgrimage headed by the bishop.

The Roman fort is the only Saxon Shore type of fortification known in the county. What remains is, in essence, a flat surface 19 ft above sea level with a depression indicating the original deep ditch dug around the walls. It was robbed of its stone to build the church, then, over the centuries, was practically ploughed away until, in 1864, work was put in hand to strengthen the sea wall. It was then that the broken seaward end of part of the wall came to light. Mr Oxley Parker, the enlightened owner of the land, ordered a careful excavation which uncovered the plan of the walls except for the eastern end which had been washed away by countless inundations. Since the area enclosed by the other three walls covers some five acres it can be seen that this impressive stonebuilt fort was an awe-inspiring deterrent to Saxons looking for loot, long before they came as settlers. All evidence of the Roman fort has gone from the site, but still the battered remains of that church stand.

The poem *Beowulf*, the only surviving secular epic in Old English, gives a brief glimpse of the life of the Saxon warriors under their Essex king. He surrounded himself with men of proven nobility, some from neighbouring kingdoms on a kind of exchange basis. He rewarded success in battle, often with gold rings, and made them see that a good weapon, well cared for, was worth more than its weight in gold. In his timber-built hall his warriors enjoyed open house and guarded his life day and night. Kings and nobles captured in battle were killed. Lesser mortals faced the fate of lifetime slavery, sold abroad if they were of the right quality. Such kings embraced Christianity as a provider of the extra power that would bring victory in battle. But it was not always a blessing – Sigbehrt, King of Essex was murdered by his own men because, as a Christian, he would keep forgiving his enemies.

Written records from the 7th century show how the 'ealdormen' – still known as aldermen down to 1974 – were responsible to the king for the administration of their areas of his kingdom. The system used the 'ten man' method of securing law and order. Men were grouped into tens and were made responsible for each other's behaviour. The lower class of Saxons were the tillers of the land in the service of their lord and the Britons who had not moved west were held as slaves or serfs, living entirely at the whim of the lord – a category which continued on, to be recorded in Domesday Book. As one historian of this period puts it: 'It was in a sense a brutally commercial society; not only did every man have his price, and every crime its compensation, but a man could sell himself, or his child, into slavery.' The precepts of the early Church had an effect on the laws issued by the king; for example, the sabbath must not be broken, and a child must be baptised within 30 days of birth.

For the first 200 years of their settlement in Essex these Anglo-Saxons used only the high value gold coins of foreign mints – the solidus and the tremissis. The solidus originated in the Roman empire as a gold coin worth originally about 25 denarii. Until decimalisation in 1971, the sloping line used to separate shillings from pence, e.g. 1/4 was still called the solidus. The tremissis was a Roman gold coin of the later emperors, said by an early 18th century expert to be worth 5 shillings

Examples of the 'sceatta' – silver coins introduced by the Saxons late in the 7th century.

sterling. Around AD 625 they imitated the latter themselves, calling it the thrymsa. Late in the same century silver coins were introduced, called 'sceattas' by modern numismatists, though their Saxon name has not been recorded. They represented that still continuing unit, the penny. The sceatta issued by the Essex kings showed the standing figure of a sphinx which, it is said, they copied from one of the ancient British coins of Cunobelin.

Civilisation and sophistication slowly developed. The new faith was a great force in that development. There were twelve bishops serving the kingdoms subject to King Aethelbald of Mercia; they were active, literate and a big influence on the Saxon kings. As one historian of the period says, '. . . they were genuinely heroes, albeit of a new type, to Anglo-Saxon society.' The new faith brought with it the book, the world-changing method of communication. Building in stone was revived, as well as stone carving. When Aethelbald was murdered by his own bodyguard in AD 757 civil war broke out, with his cousin Offa triumphant. He introduced a new approach to the lesser kingdoms like Essex, treating them as provinces of Mercia rather than as kingdoms in total thrall. Christianity was now powerful in Mercia, and also in Essex. For example, Offa asked the Pope in AD 788 for permission to reduce the province of Canterbury and set up an archbishop at Lichfield. The Diocese of Essex, up to AD 850, included minsters at St Osyth, Bradwell, Wakering, Tilbury, Barking, Upminster, Bishops Stortford and Hadstock. Offa had so increased his power that by the time of his death in AD 796 he was styled 'King of the English'.

The detailed organisation he put in place to rule this emerging unified country is glimpsed in an interesting custom dating back to his reign, first described in an ancient manuscript and repeated in Philip Morant's *History* published in 1768. In the days of the Saxon Kings, long before William the Conqueror arrived, it was necessary for the King constantly to assert his authority, and so the custom of 'Watch and Ward' was introduced. The instructions, originally written in Anglo-Saxon, have survived for that area of Essex called the Hundred of Ongar. They can be summed up as follows:

The King's Bailiff for Ongar had to cut a willow bough from Abbess Roding wood on the second Sunday after Easter. It had to be 27 in long and 8 in across. He had to take it to the Lord of the Manor of Rookwood Hall, wrapped in a fine linen cloth and then lay it on a cushion in the Lord's own apartments. Then, when the Bailiff had relieved and refreshed himself (as explicitly stated in the instructions) he was to take the Wardstaff, as it was now to be called, to Long Barns, still so named today, where all the lords, landowners and tenants who held their land by service to the King had been ordered to gather together, bringing with them all the armed retainers they would have to provide for the King's service in time of war. All through the night this host of people subservient to the king had to 'watch and keep ward in due silence' as a gesture of loyalty to king and country.

Here, at Long Barns in Abbess Roding, a thick rope was drawn waist-high across the road, with a bell tied to one end, so that if an intruder tried to creep along the lane at dead of night he would hit the rope, ring the bell and thus alarm the watchers. But as the years passed and the risk of civil war receded it is likely that the all-night vigil degenerated into jolly carousing.

The old barns at Rookwood Hall Farm, Abbess Roding, where the 'watch and ward' ceremonies for the Essex Hundred of Ongar took place.

46

As soon as the sun rose, the precious wardstaff would have a notch cut in it; then it was reverently passed on to the next 'Hundred' centre and the whole process was repeated. How did it all end? Has such a wardstaff survived? Morant says, 'To conclude, this Wardstaff was to be carried through the Towns and Hundreds of Essex, as far as a place called Atte wode near the Sea, and be thrown there into the Sea. This custom hath been long neglected.' It is not surprising therefore that not one of these 'wardstaffs' exists in England today.

Saxon craftsmanship in wood is shown in the relics of their work in the fabric of the church of St Andrew's at Greensted-juxta-Ongar. Its original walls were made of the material the Saxons found most readily to hand, wood from the forest which was then the great provider of fuel, building material, wild animals and the place to feed their pigs. Vast trunks of oaks, the like of which we will not see again, were split in three down their length. Keyed together and set in a cill of a similar beam lying directly on the soil, they made the walls. Scientific tests have set the date of the construction at around AD 850. In addition to this church and that of St Peter on the Wall at Bradwell, there are at least a dozen churches in Essex still retaining proof of their Saxon lineage.

The Saxons, successful invaders slowly working towards a unified rule over the English part of the island, were in their turn harried and hunted by the Danes whose continual raids could only be bought off to relieve the folk on the eastern seaboard. Essex was one of the counties where the 'Danelaw' was in operation and vast sums had to be raised to placate the rapacious Danes. The Saxon kingdoms were still evolving as can be seen in the *Anglo-Saxon Chronicle*, written almost day by day as events occurred. Described by F M Stenton in *Anglo-Saxon England* as: 'a series of annals written in English, intended to give a West Saxon reader of King Alfred's time an outline of history,' it looks back to the invasion of Britain by the Romans, gives a sketch of events down to AD 449, then continues as an original source of contemporary events.

We read how Essex lost its autonomy in AD 825 when Egbert, King of the West Saxons (Wessex) fought and defeated Beornwulf, king of the Mercians, and then sent a detachment into Kent that not only defeated its king, Bealdred but also effected the submission of all the South Saxons (Sussex) and the East Saxons (Essex). Battles continued, power swayed to and fro as enemies switched sides and new alliances were formed. Egbert died in AD 839 and installed his son as ruler over Kent, Essex, Surrey and Sussex. The Danish raids continued far into King Alfred's time.

The connections with the Church were not cut by these endless wars. In AD 890 the *Chronicle* reports: 'In this year Abbot Beornhelm took to

47

St Andrew's at Greensted-juxta-Ongar, famous throughout the county for its Saxon nave. Constructed in about AD850, the original walls were built from great trunks of oak, split in three down their length and set in a beam lying on the soil.

Rome the alms of the West Saxons and of King Alfred,' and in AD 893 it spoke of yet another Danish raid: '. . . they captured much booty, and wished to carry it across the Thames into Essex, to meet the ships.' They lost the next battle and Alfred recovered the booty. It was at Benfleet around AD 893, where Haesten the Dane had a great camp built, that a small English force was victorious. They burnt or destroyed the Danes' ships and took them all to London. Haesten's wife and two sons were brought triumphantly to Alfred but he released them because of the 'godson' relationships which had sprung up between Saxon and Dane under the influence of the Church. Response from the Danes was a further ravaging of the Essex countryside. At Shoebury two Danish armies were assembled prior to an assault up the Thames and along the Severn. In AD 894 Danes camped on Mersea Island then sailed and rowed round to the Thames and up to the Lea, thus circumscribing three of the borders of the present county.

5

DANELAW AND THE VIKINGS

In AD 899 Alfred died and the *Chronicle* reported: 'He was king over the whole English people except for that part which was under Danish rule . . .' There was a determined attempt to evict the Danes. In the spring of AD 912 King Edward headed a strong force which went into Essex and camped at Maldon while the 'borough' or fortification was being made at Witham – 'and a good number of the people who had been under the rule of the Danish men submitted to him.' Four years later, 'King Edward went to Maldon and built and established the borough before he went away.' With Essex under Danish control it was an obvious target for English raids. In AD 917 a great army of English coming up from Surrey and Kent joined the Essex men in an attack on Colchester. 'Until they took it and killed all the people and seized everything that was inside – except the men who fled . . . over the wall.' Later that same year King Edward took an army of West Saxons to Colchester and had the fortifications repaired. Crowds of people who had suffered terrible privation for 30 years under the Danelaw came to pledge their loyalty to the king. The whole army of East Anglia submitted to him as their rightful commander. There were more than a few Danes who joined in this declaration of fealty.

By the end of October AD 940 Edmond, son of Edward, had been consecrated as king and continued the campaign against the Danish occupation of East Anglia, but he was dead by AD 946, stabbed by a traitor. Eventually, in AD 959 Edgar became king – '. . . in his day things improved greatly, and God granted him that he lived in peace as long as he lived' as the *Chronicle* puts it. He died in AD 975. Essex comes into the picture again when the *Chronicle* informs us in AD 991, 'In this year Olaf came with 93 ships to Folkestone, and ravaged round about it, and from there went to Sandwich, and so from there to Ipswich, and overran it all, and so to Maldon. And ealdorman Brihtnoth came against him there with his army and fought against him; and they killed the ealdorman there and had control of the field. And afterwards peace was made with them and the king stood sponsor to him afterwards at his confirmation.' Another version of the *Chronicle* informs us that 'in that year it was determined tribute should be paid to the Danish men because of the great terror they were causing along the coast. The first payment was 10,000 pounds.' In August 1991 a modern 'Chronicle', the *Essex Chronicle*, reported: 'History repeated itself in Maldon at the weekend with a spectacular battle re-enactment of that fateful event 1,000 years ago when sword clashed sword and the bloodied bodies of brave warriors fell . . . . It was the same day – August 11, 991 AD when Anglo Saxon warriors gathered to defend their country against Viking invaders.' The real battle was a disaster for the Saxons, or the English as they might be called by then.

The reason for their terrible defeat was this: the Danes had camped on Northey Island in the Blackwater estuary where there has always been a tidal causeway across to the mainland. Instead of picking off the Danes individually as they streamed across the causeway, the English let them come across and form up in battle array. They decimated the English, collected their booty and sailed away triumphantly. This was but a minor incident in Essex history. We would not have known about it had not a Saxon minstrel survived to compose a long song about it which he sang in the halls of Saxon chiefs all around the county of the

A re-enactment in 1991 marking the millennium of the disastrous Battle of Maldon.

East Saxons. His song is treasured as one of the oldest English poems, though its Anglo-Saxon words make it incomprehensible. Luckily, it has been translated and can be enjoyed in modern English.

An aerial view of Northey Island. In AD991 the Danes camped here and were able to cross the causeway unmolested by the English. Once formed in battle array, they were unstoppable.

In AD 994 Essex was once again subjected to 'burning, ravaging, and slaying' as Olaf Tryggvason and Swein Forkbeard, King of Denmark, blackmailed the English for a further tribute of £16,000. Hostages were exchanged during a peace treaty, then Olaf was confirmed, his sponsor King Ethelred showered gifts on him, and he promised he 'would never come back to England in hostility.' But other Danes continued their very profitable raids, Forkbeard prominent among them. The only thing that stopped their ravaging of East Anglia in 1005 was the great famine affecting the whole of England. So scarce was food that the Danish raiders actually went home 'and let a little time elapse' before they came back. In 1009 the Danes raided in the south all summer then took up their winter quarters on the Thames and lived off Essex and the adjacent shires. Two years later the *Chronicle* recorded that they had overrun Essex again. It actually named 14 other counties in the south and east which had suffered the frightful pillaging and cruelty of the Danes. Even the Archbishop of Canterbury was captured and martyred.

In 1014, when that fearsome Forkbeard died, Ethelred felt it wise to re-confirm his kingship of all England, though the men who manned the fleet had elected Cnut the Dane, whose army was then centred on Gainsborough. Ethelred made a surprise attack on it, but Cnut escaped aboard one of his ships. In this year there was a great tide, and Essex would certainly have felt the brunt of it. '. . . the sea flooded widely over this country, coming up higher than it had ever done before, and submerging many villages and a countless number of people' as the chronicler of the day puts it. Ethelred died on St George's Day (23rd April) 1016 and Edmund was declared king. He tackled Cnut and drove off his marauders. As they retreated they laid waste to Essex once again, heading for Mercia. The treachery endemic in those times is shown in the *Chronicle*'s account. 'When the king learnt that the army had gone inland, for the fifth time he collected all the English nation; and pursued them and overtook them in Essex at the hill which is called Ashingdon, and they stoutly joined battle there. Then Ealdorman Eadric did as he had often done before; he was the first to start the flight . . . and thus betrayed his liege lord and all the people of England. There Cnut had the victory and won for himself all the English people.'

Peace was arranged and ransom was paid after a meeting of the kings. Edmund died shortly afterwards and Cnut was the obvious choice to succeed him. To strengthen his position Cnut married Ethelred's widow. In 1020 he and his archbishops, bishops, earls and courtiers came to Ashingdon in a great crowd and consecrated the minster he had ordered to be built in celebration of that victory which brought him the throne. He made a lasting peace with his fellow Danes, which held to his death in 1035. A C Edwards is cautious about the identification of the site of this battle: '. . . some historians think it was fought at Ashingdon; others favour Ashdon in north-west Essex, with Hadstock church near by as the minster which Canute built to commemorate his victory.'

After much skulduggery Harold was chosen as king and he was followed quickly by his half brother Hardacnut, who died in 1042, when Edward the Confessor came to the throne. He married Edith, daughter of Earl Godwine, a powerful man who had Cnut to thank for his advancement. 1046 was remembered in Essex, as elsewhere, for a terrible winter, 'so hard a winter as that was, both for pestilence and murrain, and birds and fish perished through the great cold and through hunger.' We know also from this same source, the *Anglo-Saxon Chronicle*, that Walton-on-the-Naze was the scene of a minor naval invasion by the outlawed Danish pirate Osgood Clapa.

In one of many struggles for power, Earl Godwine and all his sons were driven out of England in 1051. Some went to Bruges, Harold to Ireland, and from these bases they made raids on the English and Welsh coasts. The quarrel was soon patched up, the family forgiven and restored to their positions and possessions and Harold succeeded to the earldom in 1053. The expanding influence and power of the Church is reflected in the constant reference to the journeyings of archbishops and bishops in the *Chronicle*. Harold showed his fitness for kingship by subduing the Welsh in a series of battles. His reward came when Edward died on 5th January 1066, and he was chosen as king. His connection with Essex had begun when he was appointed its 'governor' and continued with his founding of the Abbey at Waltham on the directions of Edward the Confessor, as a condition attached to the gift of Waltham as a manor to Harold. In 1062 a college for a dean and 11 secular canons was founded and richly endowed by Harold with

The magnificent Waltham Abbey, first established as a 'college' by King Harold in 1062 and confirmed as an abbey by Henry II in 1177, as an act of atonement for the murder of Thomas à Becket.

land from the manor and from others in Essex and beyond. It stayed in this form, though deprived of much of its property by William the Conqueror, until 1177 when Henry II translated it into an abbey, with an abbot and 16 monks replacing the secular canons, as an act of expiation for the murder at Canterbury of Thomas à Becket. It flourished right up to its closure at the Reformation as a body answerable only to the King and the Pope, with 27 abbots covering a span of 362 years. Harold is said to have prayed here on his way south to the Battle of Hastings, and after interment near the field of battle his body was dug up and taken reverently to Waltham for burial in his abbey.

The original foundation of the Abbey predating Harold's 'College' had been credited to Tovi, Cnut's brave standard-bearer, about whom there is a local legend. A blacksmith at Montacute in Somerset was told in a dream to get the priest and the villagers to dig a great hole in the hill above the village, where they would find treasure. They dug, and they found a huge rock cleft in twain; inside it was an image of Christ on the cross in glittering black flint. The local Lord, Tovi le Prude, knew this was a sign from God. He had the heavy cross hoisted on to a huge waggon harnessed to 12 red oxen and 12 white cows.

He said they would go wherever God willed and prayed for guidance. To the beasts he called out one holy place of pilgrimage after another, from Glastonbury to Winchester, but the animals did not move. He then mentioned the little settlement in the forest of Essex called Waltham, where he was building a country retreat, and the waggon moved as if it was pushing the beasts. Off they set and every day the oxen and the cows were eager to press on with the pilgrimage until they came at last to Waltham, where they could not be urged on further. A wondering crowd helped to unload the precious cross and when it was erected they saw blood flow from the side of the image of Christ. Tovi was so overcome by all that had happened that he gave all his property to the founding of communities of the Holy Cross in Waltham, Kelvedon, Loughton and Alverton, which last is probably today's Alderton Hall, Loughton. Eventually the Waltham property passed into Harold's hands and the building of a magnificent church was put in hand. What we see today is the rebuilding of 1242, with later repairs and additions.

Harold then was King; and hearing that Count William of Normandy, King Edward's kinsman, was intending to invade England and take power, he amassed the greatest land and sea forces yet seen in this country. When this threat of invasion diminished, Harold stood down this very expensive army. The threat then came from the north with a huge invasion force under King Harold of Norway landing in the Ouse to do battle with the English at Stamford Bridge – two pitched battles within five days after a forced march north. William saw his chance and made a landing at Pevensey Bay, advanced to Hastings and forced the inhabitants to help his army build fortifications. At the Battle of Hastings Harold was killed, William became king and a new era began.

Before passing from Saxon to Norman Essex, let us consider the reminder of our Saxon heritage embodied in the County Council's coat of Arms. Permission to bear these arms, a red shield on which three seaxes are shown one above the other, with their points to the right, was granted by the College of Arms in 1932. A facsimile of the grant can be seen in the Grand Jury Room of the Shire Hall. The seax was the Saxon short sword – in use as early as the 6th century. Its symbolic use as representing the county goes back to 1770. The notch in the blades on the shield has no significance; it was introduced by the artist so that the weapon would not be confused with the scimitar. However much the seax may be considered a genuine Saxon accoutrement, a complete example has not yet been found in Essex.

Essex was soon honoured by a visit from William. It happened in this way: at his coronation at Westminster on Christmas Day in 1066 when the people gave a great shout of acclamation, the Norman guards thought this was the beginning of an insurrection and they set fire to all the buildings round the abbey to flush out the rebels. The congregation rushed out of the church and King and clergy were left wondering what was happening. William immediately set out for the safety of the nunnery at Barking Abbey and put in hand work to defend London if there was such an insurrection. So it was at Barking that he received in submission the Saxon earls like Edwin, Morcar and others who had come down from the north. Here he also drew up London's charter.

This famous Benedictine Abbey had been founded in the 7th century. Apart from the parish churches which had risen rapidly in the county, the only religious foundations preceding the Conqueror's reign were St Cedd's missionary centre at Ythancestir, Bradwell-on-Sea, where the evangelising bishop gathered round him Essex men to train as priests and laity in the new churches established from the 7th century onwards; at Tilbury where he founded one of the first monasteries; Harold's notable College of Canons at Waltham; and the legendary nunnery of St Osyth.

By William's time the Church was highly organised. The *Victoria County History* of Essex puts it neatly: '. . . the incidental and indirect evidence of the presence of pre-Conquest churches all over the area of this populous and busy kingdom of the East Saxons is abundant.' In Colchester there were six churches, although only two are mentioned in the Domesday survey. The dedications of a dozen or more churches indicate their pre-Conquest origin. The lands in Essex which by then had been ceded to the mother church of St Paul's in London were widespread. Imagine the discomfort suffered by the Dean of St Paul's in the winter of 1181 when he had to travel on a week-long circuit of inspection of churches at Belchamp, Wickham, Kirby-le-Soken, Heybridge, Tillingham, Runwell, Barling, Norton, Navestock and Chingford.

At Barking, the Abbey was founded in AD 666, as a Benedictine nunnery. Erkenwald, son of Offa, is thought to have been the founder, prior to his elevation to the Bishopric of London. The money for the endowment was given by the princes of the East Saxon kingdom. There are large gaps in the history of this foundation, some of them due to the ravaging of the Danes. In AD 870 these pagan raiders came up the Thames and burned to death all the nuns in their own church. It was this gross act which caused the Abbey to be vacated and neglected for over a hundred years, until returned by King Edgar to its former degree of importance. William the Conqueror confirmed its charter in 1066.

In 1279 the Bishop of London held an inquiry into the daily running of the Convent and tightened up on its discipline: 'No man, under pain of excommunication, shall ever go into the nuns' rooms . . . and except at confession no nun shall speak alone to a man . . . .' When a disastrous flood ruined its Thames-side properties, necessitating expensive repairs, the Abbey never seemed to recover its former prosperity. Its dissolution on 14th November 1539 was uneventful and it was demolished in 1541. The only evidence of that great foundation left is the Fire Bell, or Curfew Tower, which was not built until 1370. It was originally a gate-tower with a rood loft over the arch. Three holy figures can still be seen, though they are very worn. The outline of the abbey church foundations is indicated by lines of stone set in the turf adjacent to the parish church.

To return to our narrative: in 1077 it was reported that the summer was so dry that 'wildfire came upon many shires and burned down many villages; and also many towns were burned down.' As Essex is on the dryest side of the country, and as most houses and churches at that time were built of timber straight from the forest it can be imagined how hard the county was hit. It is quite likely that the coastal regions of the county were laid waste in 1085 as William followed a 'scorched earth' policy against a projected invasion by Cnut, King of Denmark. The threatened incursion gave William food for thought about just what this country of England meant to him, how much it was worth fighting for and to what extent losses in men and materials would be justified. 'Then he sent his men over all England into every shire and had them find out how many hundred hides there were in the shire, or what land and cattle the king himself had in the country, or what dues he ought to have in twelve months from the shire.' So we come to the Domesday survey – the first detailed account of Essex as a separate county.

6

THE CONQUEROR'S KINGDOM

The author of the *Anglo-Saxon Chronicle* spoke in what might be termed reluctant admiration of the great Survey: '. . .so very narrowly did he have it investigated, that there was no single hide nor virgate of land nor indeed . . . one ox nor one cow nor one pig which was there left out, and not put down in his record; and all these records were brought to him afterwards.' A modern commentator on our county, H C Darby, has said: 'Essex occupies a special place among Domesday counties. On the one hand, it is described in the Little Domesday Book, and it has, therefore, much in common with Norfolk and Suffolk. Its entries are far more detailed than those of the counties described in the main Domesday Book.'

The Book shows that the area of the county of Essex has changed little in more than 900 years; three villages, Great and Little Chishall and Heydon were transferred to Cambridgeshire in 1895 and Ballingdon and Brundon were transferred to Suffolk in 1905. Domesday includes around 440 places, but that does not allow for all those villages which include the same generic name, like the nine Roding villages, of which there are now eight, and the three Tolleshunt settlements. Some places entered then have disappeared entirely and cannot now be identified. Others only just survive: Thunderley was a proper village with hall and church, but by 1425 it was united with Wimbish as one parish and only the house, Thunderley Hall, preserves the name. Other places are more mysterious – Dagenham was known as early as the 7th century, yet it is not recorded in Domesday and is not mentioned again in official records until 1218. Fingringhoe is also missing.

The Domesday record has been dealt with in great detail by the scholar J Horace Round in the first volume of the *Victoria County History*. The main purpose of the Survey was to put on an efficient footing the system of land tax originating in the Danegeld arrangements. In its detailed enquiry we read names and conditions of estates before and after the Conquest as they passed from Saxon lords to Norman supporters of the

Conqueror, including the classes of ruling people, landowners, farmers and peasants in a great pyramid of human activity. Then there are the remarkably detailed accounts of animals of all kinds from plough oxen right down to the one beehive which provided Springfield with its only source of sweetness, mead, and wax for the church candles.

The most important animal on every manor was the ox, harnessed to the plough in teams of eight; next we might put the pigs, so necessary that the description of the local woodland was based upon the number of pigs it would support on its 'pannage' – the acorns, beechmast and roots which made them fat and fit for the spit. In Essex particularly, the sheep was also a very special animal. The amount of pasture for sheep shown in this record indicates an industry of huge proportions. Sheep's milk, butter, cheese, wool, skins, parchment, meat and bones – all had a use. The use of the word 'wick' in so many places, especially round the coast, shows how the 'dairy' in those days went to the sheep, out in the pastures, and sometimes became a hamlet in its own right.

Many of the saltpans from pre-Roman days were still used. They are entered under 22 separate places – and not just one apiece: Totham had seven, the three Tolleshunts a total of 13. Salcote, the only parish in England to be named after its salt-making, did not have a saltpan when the Conqueror's clerks rode in to make their survey. All they would have seen was a wide-spreading Red Hill. It is hard to imagine saltworks at Wanstead but it is there in the record.

Fishing was another industry by which the local people gained a hard-won living. Fishing on the coast and up the rivers related to 'weirs' situated on the lord's land and water, subject to his exploitation. The weirs were made of woven wattle zig-zagging into a bottle-basket end so that tidal ebbing or undamming of the river produced the harvest. Even the village of Springfield had a fishery on the Chelmer.

The mills mentioned were watermills. The earliest references to windmills are found in the last 20 years of the 12th century, while the watermill was invented shortly before the birth of Christ. For 1,000 years the watermill beside or bestriding the stream was a focal point in at least a third of all the Essex settlements shown in Domesday; in the rest, corn still had to be ground by the primitive handmill or quern. While most people were drinking the water from the rivers where fish swam, the Norman lords were quick to plant vineyards on their newly acquired properties to provide the wines they were accustomed to back home. Some of the vines had not reached maturity when the Survey was taken. One that had was at Rayleigh where Suain had raised his castle mound. The entry says there were at that time six 'arpents' of vineyard which yielded 20 'muids' of wine 'in a good season.' This is the only vineyard in the whole survey to have its yield specifically stated though in foreign terms. Aubrey de Vere had planted a vineyard of the same size at Castle Hedingham and it is claimed that some of those grapes could still be seen, growing wild, some 700 years later. He probably had another house at Belchamp Walter, for there he put in hand an even more extensive vineyard. There was another at Great Waltham which we can presume had been planted by Geoffrey de Mandeville for he had his castle at Pleshey, the adjoining parish.

The universal man-made feature, seen in almost every settlement, was the church, yet it gets no mention at all but for 17 sites out of the 440 entries. The simple answer is that few churches provided revenue to the crown. As with worship so with trade. Markets had been established as the concomitant of expanding urban life, yet there is no reference at all to a market in Essex. Round explains: 'Of the industries and sources of wealth Domesday can tell us little, for these at the date of the great Survey were primitive and few.'

Even Colchester's entry does not include a reference to its market. It is devoted in the main to the holders of land and houses, from whom money would be forthcoming. The size of the town can be judged from the fact that some 404 houses are recorded. With the addition of those houses listed under their out-of-town owners, the total could come to about 420, which was a big town in those days. The population has been estimated at well over 2,000, with many living in the merest hovels. We know that Colchester still had a mint for it is recorded that the value to the crown was £40, to be divided with Maldon which also had a mint. That town is covered in six separate entries under the various owners of the land, but, once again, without details of its shipping and commercial business. The accent, again, is on the agriculture – eleven ploughs in use, ten acres of meadow, wood for 80 pigs, pasture for 200 sheep and so on. The inhabitants are classified from freemen to bottom-of-the-pile serfs, but adding them together produces only 42 people. The town houses were all owned by the King. It seems they had no land attached. Despite the small number recorded, it has been estimated that the population was really around 1,100, responsible between them for providing a horse for the army and a ship for the navy when required.

Chelmsford's entry shows that it was wholly in the hands of the Bishop of London. Moulsham was a separate hamlet then owned by the Abbot of Westminster. There was much meadow where the Can and Chelmer flooded uncontrolled but in the vales of these two rivers there was land good enough to keep seven plough teams at work, two on the Bishop's own lands and five for the rest of land tilled by the people in co-operative endeavour, paying their rent to the Bishop in labour and other services. The Roman bridges by this time had disintegrated. Wading the ford was the only means of crossing a river and winter flooding simply cut off trade and travel. Moulsham, on the other side of the river, had been where the Romans settled, and it was still more valuable in terms of annual income to the King. Chelmsford rated £8, Moulsham £12, Writtle, a large royal manor, over £100.

Other entries in the great book reveal how might was right in those days, when powerful lords could torture and put to death at their merest whim anyone who offended them. Odo, Bishop of Bayeux, a fighting bishop if ever there was one, benefited greatly from William's generous gifts of lordships; he also used his influence and the strength of armed retainers to take over other land. But it was his under-tenant Ralf, son of the Turold shown in the Bayeux tapestry, who showed greater greed, seizing whole manors as well as the plots of humble freemen. In East Hanningfield he drove 22 such men from the land they held of Ely Abbey. He took much more from Barking Abbey, driving off the tenants as if he were brushing off flies.

Other landowners, apart from church and crown, included the great barons like Geoffrey de Mandeville and Aubrey de Vere. The Mandevilles ruled 12,000 acres of land around Pleshey Castle. Unusually, their title of Earl of Essex could pass in the female as well as the male line, so when the Earl died in 1189 without male issue, it continued in the female line until 1373. Their lands stretched out through the Leighs, the Chignals, Broomfield, Barnston and as far as the Rodings. His grateful sovereign also granted Geoffrey land at Walden, before it had the prefix 'Saffron', where he built another grand house, and endowed a priory which became an Abbey in 1190.

Aubrey de Vere owned estates in Cambridgeshire and Suffolk but made his headquarters at Hedingham, in a castle which is still impressive as a ruin. The greatest land-owning Baron in Essex was Count Eustace of Boulogne, who held court at Witham. Forty years after his properties were detailed in Domesday his heiress married the man who was to be King Stephen, so all these estates passed into royal possession.

This ancient official record does show some very human aspects. Looking in the Essex telephone directories, you will see that there are a number of people named Godsave, Godsafe or Godsalve – a family name which goes all the way back to the days of the Conqueror. It sounds very religious, but look under Felsted in the Domesday Book and you will see that King William gave to 'Roger dominus salvaet dominas' land in that area. Translate that name and you will find it means 'Roger, God-save-the-ladies.' Such a naughty Norman knight looked so handsome in all the trappings of war that it is not surprising that he had quite a few descendants!

The Domesday Book gave William full knowledge of the kingdom he had conquered 20 years before. But all that work, carried out so carefully, gave him no pleasure or profit for he died in the same year it was completed – 1086. Bearing in mind the great forest of Essex in which kings and nobles continued hunting through the centuries, the epitaph for William in the Anglo-Saxon *Chronicle* is apt:

'He made great protection for the game
And imposed laws for the same,
That who so slew hart or hind
Should be made blind.

He preserved the harts and boars
And loved the stags as much
As if he were their father.
Moreover, for the hares did he decree that they should go free.
Powerful men complained of it and poor men lamented it,
But so fierce was he that he cared not for the rancour of them all,
But they had to follow out the king's will entirely
If they wished to live or hold their land,
Property or estate, or his favour great.'

It has been said that 'There is no county perhaps that bears more clearly than Essex the imprint of the Norman Conquest' (Round). Two places have French names – Beaumont and Pleshey, the latter showing evidence of occupation by the Ancient British, Romans, Saxons and Normans. Once it was called Tumblestown because of the old entrenchments and the tumuli. The Normans gave it the name that stuck, Pleshey, meaning a fortification made by growing a thick hedge, like the prickly blackthorn, and bending it back on itself by interlacing the branches. Many more places show the hand of the new Norman lord heavy upon them in the prefixes applied to the old names. For example, the wide-spreading parish of Woodham was split amongst the new king's favourites. First the noble Ferrers and later barons Mortimer and Walter received a share. The Layer villages were similarly divided between king's men Marney, Breton and de la Haye. Norton Mandeville reflects its ownership by the Earl of Essex.

For the continuing story of the county in the first half of the 12th century we can quote the historian David Coller, writing in 1861, 'Under Henry I (1100–1135) and the usurper Stephen (1135–1154) Essex lay in the sullen quietude of despotism. In the time of the latter, whose Queen

61

Hedingham Castle – a beautiful example of a Norman Keep, towering 100 ft. The surrounding grassland was where the inner bailey defences once stood.

died at Hedingham Castle in 1152, little is recorded of the county.' In one of the many power struggles between Norman barons and the King, Roger Bigot, owner of much of Norfolk 'threw himself into the castle of Norwich and did always the worst of all throughout all the country.' His raids and depredations may well have spread into the northern part of Essex, including Colchester. For years the struggle persisted as baron after baron was besieged in his castle and winkled out by starvation. It all cost money, as the *Chronicle* reports: '. . . in the course of these proceedings, this country was severely injured by unjust taxes and many other misfortunes.' Neither side considered the plight of the peasantry. The local barons were despots but when the King and his men arrived to confront them, '. . . there was complete ravaging of his wretched people caused by his court, and in the course often burnings and killings.'

The burden of floods have been endured by Essex ever since it existed, but in 1114 the chronicler reported just the opposite, an ebb tide so far receding that Essex people east of London bridge could actually paddle across to the Kentish bank. In Stephen's reign, 1135 to 1154, the land-owning barons thought to defend their land and positions by building castles and retaining their own private armies. 'I have neither the ability nor the power to tell all the horrors nor all the torments they inflicted upon wretched people in this country and that lasted the nineteen years while Stephen was king and it was always going from bad to worse . . .' It was said then that if two or three men happened to come riding in to a village all the folk would flee in terror, assuming that they were robbers – from the royal court or from the barons.

The everyday life of these times has been likened by L C Latham to an illuminated initial seen in a medieval manuscript. It showed the three figures typical of this age – the tonsured clerk, the knight in full armour, and the peasant in his humble homespun, leaning on a spade. The three of them represent the deep divisions of feudal society: the monk at his prayers, the knight ruling by his sword and the poor peasant producing the food, shown in the illustration by his shrinking subservient posture as acknowledging his inferior status compared with those men of learning and of power. 'Although he and his like constituted the broad basis on which society rested in an age when practically every man's status, whatever his occupation, was derived from his relation to, and from the extent of his possession of land.'

The practice of communal agriculture originated far back in the Anglo-Saxon period; from it such labourers had inherited the 'open field' system with individual holdings often widely scattered. All the hard-pressed Essex peasants, pawns of warring knights and bishops, had to depend on the lords to whom they were tied from birth by shackles of service and by the need for protection. There must have been terrible tension in the relationship between those peasants of Saxon stock and their new lords from Normandy, who had summarily dispossessed almost all their former Saxon masters.

There is no doubt that Essex must have suffered from the lawlessness of Stephen's time, yet we can read of one most peaceful corner of the county, tucked away in the forest wilderness of Highwood. The site is still known locally as Bedeman's Berg. Behind Monk's and Barrow's Farm at Highwood is an enclosure in which can be seen the last crumbling remains of an ancient wall, the only remnant of a little chapel attached to a hermitage on a hill where the hermit, the 'man of prayer' lived. Bedeman means a man of prayer and Berg is the hill. The site was chosen carefully, with a spring of good water nearby and it is still called Holy Well to this day.

A replica of a siege tower (left) and catapult (right), part of the reconstructions at Stansted Mount-fitchet, where the original keep, destroyed in 1215, has been recreated as a tourist attraction.

The first hermit, called Robert, petitioned King Stephen for this land from his forest, and for the materials to build his chapel and his dwelling. The King agreed on condition that the hermit prayed every day for whichever king was on the throne, and for the souls of those departed, for ever. Stephen could not know that within 400 years Henry VIII would have all religious houses closed, from Highwood's humble hermitage to Colchester's magnificent St John's Abbey. By 1544 the land had passed into the hands of the Petre family and a little heap of stone is all that is left to remind us of that happy hermit Robert praying daily for his king.

At least 14 castles in Essex were listed. At Pleshey, where there is evidence of continued occupation from prehistoric times, there is a motte and bailey castle which would have had a timber fortification on an elliptical mound some 900 ft in diameter. It was built for Geoffrey de Mandeville shortly after the Conquest. At Saffron Walden he rebuilt the castle on a mound, originally fortified by Anscar, master of horse to Edward the Confessor, adding a keep of flint rubble, only the merest fragments of which survive. Of the castle which gave Hedingham its prefix, Pevsner is very enthusiastic '. . . one of the mightiest and most famous of East Anglia, it was built by, and belonged to, one of the most powerful families of Norman England, the de Veres, Earls of Oxford.' Built about 1135 of Barnack stone, it is the best preserved tower-keep

64

in England. This family also had a timber keep erected on a 45 ft high mound at Great Canfield, soon after 1066. Its moat is still supplied by a tiny tributary of the Roding.

Stansted Mountfitchet's castle has been reconstructed from the ancient remnants as a tourist attraction. A few original stones indicate the possibility of a stone keep erected in the 12th century by the Mountfitchet/ Gernon family, whose line failed in 1258. It would seem that the castle keep was destroyed in 1215 in accordance with Magna Carta. Chipping Ongar's castle was built by the de Lucy family in the first half of the 12th century and its last remains were pulled down in the second half of the 16th century. Clavering castle even a hundred years ago was represented only by its earthen mound and excavations, though its keep had been built of stone. It is thought that it was erected before the Conquest, with a complicated system of moats and a reservoir designed to drive a mill – an early Essex example of hydraulic engineering.

Rayleigh's castle mound was raised on a spur of the hills which overlook the flat land away to the west. The note in the Domesday

The last vestiges of a magnificent castle – Hadleigh seen from the air today. It was ruined not by desperate battle but by land subsidence and the removal of the stone by a later owner for other building projects.

65

Book that 'in this manor Swein built his castle' suggests that this was one of the earliest castles raised after the Conquest, though it is possible that the earthworks are older and were simply taken over and adapted by the Normans. It must have been an early construction for no stones have been found on the site. In the volume of the *Victoria County History* published in 1903 a footnote warns: 'With sorrow we have to advise those who wish to see Rayleigh Castle to do so speedily, for the destroyer is at hand; already roads are marked out on the western slope, and soon the grand view will (thanks to modern vandalism) be changed to a prospect of back premises of villas and cottages.'

The castle at Hadleigh was built for Hubert de Burgh in 1231, but was soon confiscated by the crown when he lost royal favour. The King took the castle over, and appointed a governor, who through several reigns had to entertain royal hunting expeditions to the deep woods all around. It was a ruin even when Constable set up his canvas to paint his famous view of the tallest remaining tower on the south-east side.

The best of all the Essex castles must be that at Colchester. It boasts the largest extant keep in Britain, measuring 151 by 100 ft at the base. It was built to the order of Eudo Dapifer, William the Conqueror's steward and confidant. He brought William Rufus across from Normandy to succeed his father. For his great help in securing Rufus on the throne he was rewarded with command of Colchester as a fortified borough, and given permission to erect a castle, as well as receiving the grant of 20 Essex manors. Towards the end of the 11th century, he put in hand the building of the castle on the site of the foundations of the great Roman temple. Originally it had at least three storeys, reached by a great spiral staircase. In the two storeys remaining can be seen two of the earliest-known fireplaces. The High Street still bends today to accommodate that ancient rampart and ditch on the south side. From quite early days the castle served as a prison, but it suffered such neglect that by 1683 John Wheeley had bought it to provide hardcore and stone for his riverside development at the Hythe. It was Charles Gray (1696–1782) who acquired it and began its repair and restoration. In 1920 it was vested in the Borough Council and now houses the important Colchester and Essex Museum which since 1860 has expanded from the crypt to fill the whole building.

These castles were a thorn in the side of King Stephen in his 'civil war' with Empress Matilda's supporters which dragged on for 15 years, to the great detriment of the folk of Essex. When Stephen died in October 1154, Henry II's succession to the throne was undisputed. He ruled an empire stretching from the Scottish border to the Pyrenees. His heart was in the centre of it, at Anjou, his native land. Of his

Built on the site of the Roman temple, Colchester Castle originally had an impressive four storeys; now reduced to two, it still boasts the largest extant keep in Britain, measuring 151 by 100 ft at the base.

reign of 34 years, 21 were spent on the continent, but he devoted much energy in bringing England to the royal heel. Castles which had been built by the barons were demolished and firm rule over Scotland and Wales was established. So much absent was he that he set up administrative arrangements to deal with finance, justice and local government on a daily basis. Here we can detect the germination of the seed of county administration. Royally appointed justices began travelling out to county centres. First they chose Writtle, then Brentwood and finally Chelmsford as the most convenient assize town. Here in 1201 the King's court granted the town its fair. The justices also had to travel to Colchester because it was written into that borough's charter that burgesses suspected of a crime must be charged within their borough. Chelmsford was chosen as the only assize town for the county in 1218, when Henry III's advisers caused a writ to be issued which confirmed a proper circuit of assize, but on rare occasions both Colchester and Rayleigh were visited to settle local cases.

Richard I died in 1199 and John succeeded him and reigned until

1216. He got into such trouble with the Pope that all church services were suspended for six years from 1208 and the following year John himself was excommunicated. He made his peace with the Pope but failed to win over his people in the war against Philip of France. Rebels captured London in May 1215. Many of these rebels would have been Essex men whose county adjoined the City. They elected Philip's son Louis as their anti-king; King John was forced to yield to the Barons' demands in the *Magna Carta* signed one year before he died in 1216, and the nine year old Henry III and his advisers had to face a civil war, with London and the south east, including Essex, in rebel hands. With two of his closest supporters, William the Marshal, now an old man, and Hubert de Burgh, he beat the French-led rebellion by land and by sea. From William's death in 1219 government largely devolved on Hubert until Henry reached his majority in 1227.

In 1231 Hubert saw his castle at Hadleigh completed. A year later King Henry, now ruler in his own right, fell out with Hubert, stripped him of all his properties and forced him to flee persecution. Hubert first claimed sanctuary at Merton Priory, then at the chapel in Brentwood built for his nephew, the Bishop of Norwich in 1216. Here the soldiers caught up with him, but holding the cross in one hand and the host, the holy bread of communion, in the other, he claimed sanctuary. The soldiers laughed at the idea and dragged him out. The local blacksmith was called to make fetters for him, but, so the legend goes, the smith recognised Hubert, threw down his tools and said, 'As the Lord liveth, I will never make iron shackles for him; but will rather die the worst death there is. God be judge between him and you for using him so unjustly and inhumanly.' So the soldiers tied Hubert's legs under his horse's belly with cords, bound his arms and took him off to imprisonment in the Tower of London. The story is not a total tragedy; some of Hubert's property was returned to him on his release and he was allowed to live in retirement for the last eleven years of his life.

The great power gained by the Church by the 12th century is shown in the catalogue of its possessions in the Domesday survey. When vicarages were established, largely from the 13th century, the incumbents were given the benefit of all the small tithes, which excluded corn. This meant that of all goods, food and related products grown or made in the parish one tenth was to be yielded up to the vicar, who used them as he thought best for the benefit of his living and of the church. The system of paying tithes was commuted to a money payment in the years either side of 1840. It resulted in the preparation of extremely detailed maps and 'awards' which are still in the Essex Record Office.

There were some unusual incidents to enliven the story of the developing Church. Some time in the first decade of the 14th century Bishop Baldock had to enquire into the happenings at Ashingdon church. There were rumours that an image, probably of the Virgin, had power to work miracles, especially in the case of barren women, and crowds of people came from far and near, hoping to gain relief from all kinds of sickness, as well as to ensure conception. The rector was making a good income from the pilgrims much to the disgruntlement of neighbouring clergy whose own takings were falling away. At almost the same time a similar superstition grew up at Rayne, where another image of the Virgin was held to work miracles for expectant mothers. Even a century later, pregnant women were still making their pilgrimage to the church to pray for their own successful pregnancy and prompt delivery.

The wonderful late 15th century Grange Barn in Coggeshall, with its beautiful timber work successfully restored by the County Council, was used for storing tithes for the church.

The story of the religious houses from foundation to final closure during the Reformation is comprehensively set out in one of the early volumes of the continuing *Victoria County History*. A D Bayne has counted them thus: 2 mitred abbeys, 6 common abbeys, 22 priories, 3 nunneries, 3 colleges, 2 preceptories of Templar knights and 9 leper hospitals. It was in the last-named, at Colchester, Bocking, Brook Street, South Weald, Castle Hedingham, Hornchurch, Ilford, Newport and Maldon, that the monks and nuns followed most closely the ideals of their various Orders in their care for the sick.

Of course monks were only human, and there were times when differences between monks and townsmen escalated into violence. At Colchester's Midsummer Fair in 1272 they clashed in a bloody confrontation. The abbot was much aggrieved; on the following day he showed the coroner a dead man in St John's Field who the monks said had been killed by the townsmen. Further questioning showed it was the corpse of a thief which had been cut down from the gallows by the monks to provide false evidence in their dispute.

It was monks and priests who first introduced education into the county, albeit for the fortunate few. Colchester Grammar School was founded before 1206. In 1464 its master was in trouble for throwing school rubbish over the town wall by the postern gate. Braintree's school began in the chantry of St John in the parish church in 1364. Here was taught John Ray, the naturalist who founded the study of botany as we know it today. He was born in 1627, and after his transfer to St Catharine Hall, Cambridge in 1644 the little school is heard of no more. Chelmsford's King Edward VI Grammar School can trace its lineage back to the foundation of a chantry 'in the chapel of our ladie in Chemysford churche yarde' in 1375, but it was in the middle of the 13th century that the first school had been established here by the Dominicans, the Black Friars, at their house in the parish of Moulsham. The King himself was interested in their work, and in 1277 he sent the large sum of ten shillings to them whilst staying at Havering. It was enough to provide a good day's food for the 30 or so brothers. It was refounded in 1551 during Edward VI's reign. Even a small place like Great Baddow had a school taught by the priest from as early as 1392, the same year in which Coggeshall's school was set up in a chantry of the church. John Jegon, Bishop of Norwich from 1602, received his pre-university education there. Maldon Grammar School is thought to have started in St Peter's church in 1388 and Saffron Walden's school was in full swing before 1423 when two chaplains were taken to court for teaching without a licence. It is possible that a small school used the chantry founded in Harlow church in 1324, and a similar foundation existed in Writtle from 1392 in 'Savall Bromefeldes alias our Ladyes Chantry.'

Henry III's battles with Simon de Montfort in 1264–65 led to the proper representation of the people in Parliament. Henry's son and heir Edward saw that this was a time for change, that the King was the stronger in the country when he ruled with the agreement of Parliament, even though it was far removed from the democratic body we know today. It was simply a King's Council where the barons could talk in general terms with the King's representatives about national matters. Henry III occasionally summoned to such meetings two or more knights elected by the Shire Court in each county to represent the county gentlemen. It was Simon de Montfort in his brief year of glory who, in 1265, summoned to London not only the representatives of the knights of the shire but also two delegates from each of the boroughs of England. The names of the Essex representatives are known only as far back as Edward's Parliament of 1290, which John le Breton and John Filiol attended.

7

MEDIEVAL ESSEX

At the opening of the 14th century the Lord of the Manor still held complete sway over the families of Essex people living and working on his land. There were still those ranks of tenants first set out in Domesday Book, though by now there were more freemen who had raised themselves to the status of what we might call yeoman farmers through generations of hard work and good husbandry. Beneath them toiled the molmen whose tenancy of their land demanded a certain number of days of labour for the lord, though by now that custom had largely fallen into desuetude. Then came the villeins who held up to 30 acres of land, followed by the coterelli with only five acres or so, and the cotmen who kept their large families off 'an acre and a cow'. The cotmen were harassed all ways – by compulsory work for their lord, by taxes for king and country, by dreadful living conditions and by plagues of incurable diseases. By the end of the 13th century most of the compulsory work for the lord and the old arrangement of payment of rents in kind had been commuted to money payment.

Under Edward I (1272–1307) Essex enjoyed the development of its markets and fairs established by royal charter. Growing towns needed these essential elements of trade though sometimes it was difficult to wrest such rights from the lord of the manor. On royal manors it was easier because the money or services required in return for the charter went straight to the king. It has been estimated that over 70 towns, some very small, gained charters for markets and fairs over the next two centuries. Colchester's charter of incorporation as a borough dates from 1189; its power to hold a market and a midsummer fair was vested in it by that same Eudo Dapifer who built the castle. Its October fair was granted by Edward II. Maldon can proudly claim that its first charter, now missing, was granted in 1171.

Chelmsford's first licence to hold a market appears to have been obtained in 1199 by the Bishop of London, Lord of the Manor, from King John. The following year a charter for an annual fair was granted. In the court held by the lord of the manor, often through his steward or agent, all the business of local government of the day was carried

Chelmsford was granted a licence to hold a market in 1199, and began to develop as the county town. This illustration shows the stone bridge at the bottom of the High Street, looking towards the old gaol before it was demolished in 1859.

out with wrongdoers 'presented' for their crimes, from larceny, and the absence from stipulated days of work for the lord, to the illegal taking in of isolated bits of manorial land or roadside 'waste' and the non-payment of the many dues owing to the lord, including, for example, the best beast from a deceased person's property, called a 'heriot'. In the Chelmsford manorial records all these matters are set down in a clear hand, with market traders and customers being entered frequently. Their places of origin, all over the county, prove the growing importance of the developing county town.

Maldon, Colchester, Brightlingsea and Harwich were important east coast ports in the 14th century. Roads in those days, and particularly on the sticky Essex clay, were no more than rough tracks, impassable for weeks and months at a time in the wet winter months, so seaborne and riverborne traffic was the most efficient. Harwich gained its first charter for self government in 1318, a sign of its early importance as the 'Gateway to Europe'. It was eventually granted two markets and two fairs. By 1352 it had been fortified – walled round against possible enemy attack as a valuable bridgehead in any invasion. Edward III and his army embarked here on the great expedition against the French in 1338.

Romford's market was granted in 1247 and it still operates, though in a modern, pedestrianised town centre. Saffron Walden was so much in the hands of the powerful Mandevilles that it could not secure the control of its own market until 1618, but the significance of the Mandevilles' market lingers in street names today, and it is possible to re-create from entries in the town books the medieval grid system of the arrangement of the stalls, set out in rows by competing merchants – Fish Row, Tanners Row, and so on. So permanent did the stalls become that they evolved into shops in their own right, which meant that stallholders of the modern age had to set out their wares in the market place itself. Thaxted's charter was not granted until 1554, long after its real importance as a centre of trade had waned. The town was famous for its cutlers, whose craft drew customers from far beyond the county. That trade lasted for some 400 years from the 12th century.

The county can claim many links with the great national events of the 14th century. For instance, Robert Bruce who secured Scottish independence by his victory over the English at Bannockburn in 1314, was born in Writtle in 1274. An ancient deed found in the church library at Hatfield Broad Oak is said to show that Bruce's parents owned valuable property there.

In 1327, when Edward III was only 15 years old, he instigated the

Romford Market, granted in 1247, pictured here at the beginning of the present century.

73

raising of a considerable contribution to the exchequer by calling for a tax or subsidy of one twentieth of the personal wealth of all people whose movable property was worth ten shillings or more. It was needed to raise and equip an army to resist the threat of invasion by Robert Bruce. The tax was to be collected county-wide, taken to Chelmsford and then sent on to Westminster as a lump sum. That would be a very complicated business today, but since the record shows that even Chelmsford at that time had only 43 people wealthy enough to qualify, the collection was manageable.

The Hundred Years' War started in 1337, ten years after Edward III came to the throne. The expedition to the Low Countries in 1338 started a new phase in the war. This, and other campaigns carried on during Edward's reign needed such vast sums of money that loans would not suffice. Essex men of some standing were called to Chelmsford to be harangued about the necessity for the war and were asked for sizable cash contributions, to be collected a fortnight later, in September 1337. However, this idea was abandoned in favour of the major towns in the county sending three or four men each to a Great Council at Westminster where, under further pressure, they voted the King a new tax on movable goods for three years. In 1340 and 1341 further swingeing taxes were introduced. More soldiers were needed as well. In 1346 Colchester had to provide 20 armed foot soldiers, and Chelmsford, Braintree, Saffron Walden and Waltham Holy Cross were also dunned in due proportion. What is more, Essex, as a county, was ordered to equip and send to the army 200 archers.

The Black Death of 1349 hit the county hard, decimating the population, and it was only one of more than 20 waves of disease which swept Essex in that century. Lack of labourers lead to the gradual breakdown of the old feudal manorial system. A new class of 'free' labourers was emerging. Sir Charles Oman explains in the *The Great Revolt of 1381*: 'The villein desiring to be quit of customary work and customary dues, in order that he may become a tenant at a fixed rent, and the landless labourer determined that at all costs he will get from his employer something more than the miserable pay allowed him by law.' John Gower, personal friend of Chaucer, writing in these troubled times said, 'Three things, all of the same sort, are merciless when they get the upper hand: a water-flood, a wasting fire and the *common multitude of small folk*. For these will never be checked by reason or discipline; and therefore, to speak in brief, the present world is so troubled by them that it is well to set a remedy thereunto.'

One of the remedies was the Statute of Labourers, proclaimed in 1350. It laid down that labourers were to serve masters at the rates obtaining prior to the plague. They could not move out of their parish to look for higher wages, and it was forbidden for anyone to give alms to able-bodied beggars; at this time the Church's teaching of charity was very influential and men found they could get more from charity than they could from honest labour. A later statute added that runaway labourers could be branded 'F' (i.e. Falsity) on their foreheads. Relations between employer and servant were so strained that for 200 years Essex was the battleground of an economic war. The stage was already set, here in Essex, for the principal acts in the drama and tragedy of the Peasants' Revolt.

'Who would ever have believed that rustics, and most inferior ones at that, would have dared to enter the chamber of the King and his mother with their filthy sticks: rebels, who had formerly belonged to the most lowly condition of serf, went in and out like lords?' That is how Thomas Walsingham put it when writing his *History of England* 100 years after the Peasants' Revolt.

What caused this sudden rising of the peasantry in 1381? Sir Richard Waldegrave, Speaker of the House of Commons at that time, blamed the extravagant life-style of the royal family and the court as perceived by the peasant, and the taxation which bore heavily on those who could least afford it. He was referring to the poll tax ordered to be collected in 1381. Such a tax was supposed to be a once-only sum of money, to be paid by everybody in the kingdom other than beggars and children, to replenish the King's coffers after drastic expenditure on wars and high living.

This was not the first poll tax. There had been one in 1377 and another in 1379. The first was only a groat, the second was three groats, and still the war was bleeding the treasury. So in 1380 Parliament was forced to approve a third poll tax, of one shilling – another three groats – on everybody over 15 years old. Essex people were very reluctant to pay it. There was no end of deception; even the people forced to be collectors fiddled the books. Parliament was not pleased. It sent out commissioners to enquire into the shortfall, and since Essex was one of the worst places for evasion they came to Brentwood on 30th May 1381 to question representatives of the parishes on the bank of the Thames, including Corringham, Fobbing and Stanford-le-Hope. They stood their ground, and when the order was given to arrest one of them the others fired off arrows at the Commissioners and wielded sticks and threw stones to drive them out of Brentwood.

That was the spark which fired the tinder of revolt. The message went round Essex that the Thameside men had thrown out the toadies of Parliament and its poll tax. A judge, Sir Robert Belknap, was sent with a military escort to Brentwood to restore law and order. The crowd gathered again in a very threatening manner so the judge rushed off back to London and safety. Rumour was rife. All around the county men formed gangs to make evident their hatred of the poll tax. From Dunmow, Coggeshall, Braintree and Bocking they came, and they took out their feelings on the country house of the King's Treasurer, Sir Robert Hales, at Cressing. He was safe in London, so they looted everything of value and set the place on fire. Men in this mob came from other places too: Barking, Brentwood, Felsted, Goldhanger, Hadleigh, the Hanningfields, Leigh and Chelmsford.

From Cressing they moved on to Coggeshall where the house of John Sewale, the King's man in this area, was burnt down. They caught and killed John Sewell, the King's 'escheator' or property agent. A new gang from Manningtree joined up with the main body who then collected all the royal and local manor records they could find and carried them to Chelmsford where, by 11th June, they were looking for the documents that Sewale kept in his house there concerning Assize and other government business. He was at home so they beat him, took all those records, piled them up in the High Street and had a great celebratory bonfire. They retained 40 or so of these documents, with their official seals in green wax attached, and tied them onto poles, carrying them as banners on their way to London. Hilda Grieve, Chelmsford's historian, called it, 'A united Essex taxpayers' protest demonstration in the centre of the County Town.'

All around the county the hard-pressed peasantry, and some men of greater substance, formed gangs, stormed manor houses and destroyed all the manor court records they could find, so that their lords could no longer lean on them with the full force of law and precedent. Chelmsford and Moulsham lost all their records before 1381 in this manner. The rebels wasted no time, for by the end of the next day they had trudged all the way to Mile End, to meet the King just outside the City of London. Richard II, then only 14 years old, went with his retinue of nobles to confront the Essex men. He negotiated with their leader and agreed that none would be punished and that conditions of service to their lords would be vastly improved.

The Essex men were well satisfied. They liked the bearing of this young king, trusted him and agreed to disperse. But some ruffians stayed to loot and pillage in London with the rebels from Kent under Wat Tyler and John Ball, who had reached London on 13th June. On the 15th these extremists met the King at Smithfield to press him still further with their demands. Everybody knows the end of the story: Wat Tyler insulted the King and was struck down by one of the nobles;

Richard II bravely rode forward, faced the noisy mob, showed them he was their king, took control – and the rebels drifted away.

The clearing up began. The King moved to Waltham Abbey to start the process, then to the royal palace at Havering and finally, on 1st July, into Chelmsford. His message there was short: 'Villeins ye are and villeins ye shall remain.' Five hundred Essex rebels shuffled into Chelmsford on that Monday, with bare feet and heads bowed in token of their penitence, and begged for mercy. They were ordered to hand over their leaders, who were tried and found guilty and around a dozen were immediately hanged on the gallows off Rainsford Road. After that the King moved on to deal with rebels from other counties. The revolt was over, the poll tax was paid, history moved on.

One strange custom practised in Essex until Elizabethan times or later had its origin in the aftermath of the Peasants' Revolt. It was known as the holding of the Lawless Court, or the Court of Cockcrowing. This court, a meeting of all the tenants of the Lord of the Manor of Rochford, was held annually, just after midnight, in the yard of a house at King's Hill, on the Wednesday after Michaelmas Day. Everybody joined a procession from the King's Head inn, with flaming torches lighting their way while the noisier element of the crowd imitated the crowing of the cock.

When they got to the courthouse everybody maintained strict silence while the steward of the court read out, in a whisper, the name of each tenant, who answered in a whisper, confirming his presence and his tenancy. Then all knelt in homage to the lord of the manor. All the business was recorded, not in pen and ink in the courtbook but with a piece of coal on a slate. Those who did not answer their whispered summons were charged heavy fines. Then the court was closed with a whisper, torches were put out as dawn lit up the scene, everybody burst into cockcrowing again – and normal life was resumed in Rochford.

Despite the heavy taxation and the hardships endured by Essex people, including the loss of hundreds of their loved ones on the battlefields of France, England eventually lost all its French possessions. By 1453 Calais was the last outpost of English occupation of French soil.

Essex suffered another, more personal insult at the hands of King Richard in 1397. In 1227 Pleshey Castle and the lordship of all its lands had passed in marriage to the Bohun family, Earls of Hereford and Essex. Within 100 years the line had failed – only two girls were left. One of them, Eleanor, was married to Thomas of Woodstock, created Duke of Gloucester in 1385. His assassination and its consequences set a blood stain on the page of Pleshey's story, as told by D W Coller in 1861:

'The Duke of Gloucester was uncle to King Richard the Second, and highly distinguished for valour, probity and honour; but having great influence in public affairs, and being opposed to the measures pursued by his nephew's favourite advisers, his destruction was determined upon, for which purpose he was treacherously decoyed from his castle of Pleshey, and forcibly conveyed to Paris, where he was murdered, in 1397.'

He died of suffocation, by being placed between two feather mattresses in the bedroom of an inn. His death was avenged, as Coller explains: 'The tenants of the Duke did not remain long without an opportunity of showing their love for their lord and their hatred of his enemies. The Duke of Exeter, who was concerned in the conspiracy, contrived to secrete himself for a while, but was at last discovered by the country people while sitting at supper in the house of a friend. He was taken first to Chelmsford, and thence, for the sake of greater security, to Pleshey, the manor of their Lord, the Duke of Gloucester. No sooner did the tenants understand that Exeter was in their power, than, resolving themselves to be the avengers of their lord, they seized upon him, and cut off his head . . .'

This grisly episode led to a mention of Pleshey in Shakespeare's 'Richard II' when Gloucester's sorrowing widow cries:

> 'With all good speed at Pleshey visit me.
> Alack, and what shall good old York there see
> But empty lodgings and unfurnished wall,
> Unpeopled offices, untrodden stones?
> And what hear there for welcome but my groans?'

During the reigns of Henry IV, V and VI, 1399 to 1461, Essex developed quietly as it became increasingly affected by the expansion of London. Henry IV confirmed to the Commons that he intended to keep the ancient laws and statutes and to 'do right to all men in mercy and in truth according to his oath.'

An unusual feature of these settled times is the way in which 'Potash' is used in the name of no less than 78 fields and six farms in Essex. Potassium carbonate, known to everybody then as 'potash', was used in washing clothes, making soap, bleaching and dyeing from the Middle Ages down to the 18th century, and all those fields and farms were sites of the shed or hut which served as the potash factory.

This potash, for all its cleaning power, was made from nothing more than ashes filtered through water, producing lye. The lye was soaked up into wheat straw which was then burned and from those ashes the black

The motte and bailey castle at Pleshey was built for Geoffrey de Mandeville shortly after the Norman conquest. The castle was later to witness the gruesome murder of the Duke of Exeter.

potash was recovered. It was just a small step from potash to soap. By 1825 the potash man had been rendered redundant.

Evidence of the ignorance and superstition rife in Essex at this time, and right down to the 17th century, is found in Holinshed's *Chronicle*, published in 1577. With belief in Satan as the doer of evil, and with no scientific explanation of natural disasters available, a simple flash of lightning caused more than a nine days' wonder in Danbury. In 1402 Danbury church, high up on that remarkable hill, was struck by lightning which raced down the spire and destroyed the nave, aisle and part of the chancel. Local folk said it was definitely the work of the devil, and it was not long before a villager was found who stoutly asserted that, just before the lightning strike, he saw the devil go into the church – in the form of a monk! So Danbury qualified for an entry in those famous *Chronicles*: 'Upon Corpus Christi day, in the year 1402, at evensong time, the Devil entered this church, in the likeness of a Grey Friar, and raged horribly, playing his parts like a Devill indeed, to the great astonishment and fear of the parishioners; and in the same houre, with a tempest of whirlewind and thunder, the top of the steeple was broken downe and half of the chancel scattered abroad.'

As to England's government in general, G M Trevelyan puts it very neatly: 'In Henry VI's reign the medieval House of Commons reached its highest point of constitutional privilege, but failed to use it for the benefit of the nation. There was no friction between Parliament and Council, because both were controlled by the same aristocratic cliques, whose only contests were against each other.' The Wars of the Roses were just such contests between the mighty barons. The fighting began in St Albans, very close to Essex, but that was the nearest it came. The intermittent battles affected other localities, but the vast majority suffered little. Trade and commerce continued as usual, with no more disturbance than the regular assault and battery from thieves and brigands.

The leading landowners of Essex, however, were much involved. For example, the Fitzlewes family of West Horndon held land in 24 locations in Essex and further increased their holdings by marriage with the de Veres, Earls of Oxford. They backed the wrong side, the Lancastrians, and were relieved of most of their Essex possessions, though some were later restored to them. The 12th Earl of Oxford (1408–1462) and his eldest son were executed because they had plotted against the King in espousing the Lancastrian cause. One family which was rewarded for loyalty was the Bourchiers, founded by John de Bourchier in Essex in the first decade of the 14th century. His eldest son was created 1st Lord Bourchier in 1330, with nearly a score of Essex manors. The barony passed down to Henry Bourchier, who was confirmed Earl of Essex and died in 1483, five days before his King, Edward IV.

The De Veres were returned to favour when the 13th Earl defended the King's cause with such bravery at the Battle of Bosworth in 1485. Henry VII heaped honours on him and he lived in splendour in the castle built by his ancestors in 1140 at Castle Hedingham. In the summer of 1498 the King went to stay there for nearly a week. As he was leaving, the Earl had all his retainers, a kind of private army, lining the road to see off the King with cheers of loyalty. The King asked the Earl if all these men were his servants. The Earl shook his head. No, he said, they were his retainers, whom he had called in from his lands all around to honour the King. The King knew that this meant they were, in fact, a private army, and since he had made a law preventing his Barons having more than a basic number of armed retainers, he thanked the Earl for his hospitality, pointed out that he was breaking the Statute of Retainers and fined him 1,500 marks – a colossal sum in the money of the day.

8

ESSEX IN TUDOR TIMES

During the 15th century, England suffered from weak kings and over-powerful subjects. As the historian L F Salzman puts it 'Looking back on England we see, just before the Tudor dynasty begins, the centre of the stage occupied by Dukes and Earls, with a chorus of retainers; in the second Act the great lords have disappeared, and the Sovereign holds the stage supported by his ministers ... Parliament, discredited in the eyes of the people, practically abdicated its authority in favour of King Henry ...' It was easier for the humblest peasant to gain an audience of Queen Elizabeth I than it would be for an ordinary citizen to get into the presence of a cabinet minister today. Yet it was Henry VIII who first assumed the title of 'Majesty' and made his courtiers bend their knee when addressing him.

We see the history of the county reflected in the development of the County Town of Chelmsford at this time. Its market was bustling with trade and many sought to benefit from the trade it engendered. In 1494 the town had been designated by Parliament as the place in the county where the official brass standard weights and measures were to be held, against which all the weights and measures used in shops and markets throughout the county had to be tried and approved.

Still more taxes were required to run the country. Henry VIII was planning an invasion of France and he needed money and soldiers. The money was to come from yet another poll tax and from a property tax. Each town was ordered to provide a proportionate number of soldiers. The account book of the borough of Maldon for 1513 shows how Baron Fitzwalter, representing the King, ordered the Borough officials to find three troopers to join the royal army and pay the cost of providing them with uniform, weapons and transport. That old book shows how the town, already hard-pressed to provide for its sick and poor, made the best of a bad job. The uniform for the troopers, a white coat with green facings, had to be bought; there was no avoiding that, but as for weapons, they took the old arms and armour off the walls of the Moot Hall, where they had been rusting away for years. They had them scoured with sand to brightness again, renewed the leather laces and

Paycocke's House in Coggeshall's West Street was begun in 1500 by John Paycocke, a wealthy local merchant, and completed after his death by his son Thomas. Paycocke's just escaped being demolished in 1890; bought and restored by Lord Buxton, it is currently owned by The National Trust.

relined the helmets. New spurs had to be bought, but they made the poor conscripts manage with old saddles. Heaven knows what condition the horses were in. There is no record surviving to tell us how the three troopers got on in their second-hand gear at the Battle of the Spurs on 15th August 1513.

Henry VIII was a regular visitor to Essex. In 1517 he bought from Sir Thomas Boleyn the house called New Hall at Boreham. It was rebuilt in the grandest style and renamed Beaulieu. He was still married to Catherine of Aragon when he so richly celebrated the Feast of St George in this house in 1524. It passed out of royal ownership in 1573, but not before it had been lived in by Queen Mary before her accession and by Queen Elizabeth, who had her arms carved over the main entrance. She granted it to Thomas Ratcliffe, Earl of Sussex. King Henry also visited the Priory at Blackmore, with such goings-on, parties and performances, all at the royal behest. It was only 25 miles from London yet buried in the countryside, where innocent pleasures could be enjoyed away from the gaze of gossips and the criticism of killjoys. Morant, the 18th century historian, says that Henry, '. . . when he had a mind to be lost with his courtesans often frequented the Priory.' It is obvious that he was doing this before the Dissolution of that priory in 1525 for it was here, in 1519 that Elizabeth Blount, one of the ladies in the retinue of Catherine of Aragon, was delivered of a son. Henry acknowledged him as his son and spoiled him thoroughly, but he died when he was 17; some said he was poisoned on the orders of Anne Boleyn. When at Blackmore, Henry made it understood that he was not to be disturbed.

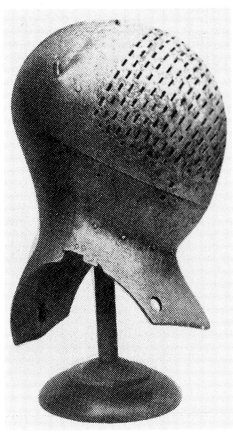

Since the house of the former Priory of St Lawrence was known as Jericho House, enquirers in London were simply told that the King had gone to Jericho – and that phrase entered general use in our language. Not many villages can claim such a distinction. The stream that fed the moat all round the priory was nicknamed the Jordan.

A sidelight on the richness of the royal life of those times is seen in the parish church at Rayne. In a glass case can be seen a knight's helm, but it is only a replica! Sir Giles Capel, Lord of the Manor, was one of the knights led by Henry VIII who, in 1520 challenged the finest knights from the continent to contests over 30 days at the Field of the Cloth of Gold, the plain near Guisnes in France. There Henry met the French king, Francois to discuss political matters on the death of Maximilian. What a grand experience that must have been for Sir Giles. Just before he died in 1556 he willed that 'my beste helmett and

The replica of the helm of Sir Giles Capel of Rayne Hall. Sir Giles' original helm was appropriated from Rayne parish church by a builder during restoration work in the 19th century and later found its way to the Metropolitan Museum of Art in New York.

my armynge Sworde be sett over my funeralls according to the devise of the harrauld.' That was the custom of the time and as a knight, he wanted them displayed correctly over his tomb, according to the heraldic conventions. They remained there for nearly 300 years. When the church was closed for six years from 1834 while it was thoroughly restored, the Capel tombs were quite unaccountably destroyed and the builder took both sword and helm as his own property! No-one knows now where the sword went but the helm was seen in the builder's workshop and bought from him for just ten shillings (50p) by a Miss Courtauld, who sent it to a friend who was interested in armour. He saw its value and sold it for a large sum to an American dealer, and so it made its way to the Metropolitan Museum of Art in New York. When that museum learned the story of the helm they presented a replica to Rayne. Without the label set beside the helm, most people would be convinced it was the original.

Great men like Sir Giles were now building houses to match their station in life. There are still more than a hundred houses in this county which began before or during the reign of Elizabeth I. It was at this time that the ancient halls, rising clear to the rafters in one large room, were partitioned horizontally and then vertically to make sets of rooms on two storeys. This status symbol of the up-and-coming man was transcended by the richer courtier who could extend his house not only upwards but outwards round one or more courtyards. Such expansion can still be seen at Panfield Hall, Horham Hall and Ingatestone Hall. As Elizabeth's reign progressed the courtyard house began to go out of fashion, supplanted by taller, more compact houses, more conveniently arranged internally, as at Eastbury House, Barking and Spains Hall, Wethersfield.

In Wolsey's time the churches were as gaudy in images, vestments, communion plate and in general decoration as the clothes which rich people were now affecting, and amongst the clergy, as in the monasteries and nunneries, there was growing laxity. Churches were used as 'museums' in which wondrous relics and strange things from foreign lands, like ostrich eggs, were put on show. The authority of the church was being challenged increasingly from the late 14th century by Wycliffe and his followers, the Lollards. Although members were hanged or burned at the stake, the movement gathered momentum as the new century opened and very late in the 15th century the King's secretary joked in a letter to Erasmus that all this burning was putting up the price of firewood.

William Tyndale's English translation of the *New Testament*, smuggled into England from a printing house on the continent in 1526, was ordered by the Bishops to be seized and thrown on the fire; but only twelve years later, after Henry VIII's break with Rome, he ordered a copy of the *Great Bible* to be rendered into English by Rogers and Coverdale, and incorporating Tyndale's work, to be placed in every church for study by the congregation. This was what led to the martyrdom of William Hunter in Queen Mary's reign.

In 1584 Richard Hakluyt wrote, '. . . through our long peace and seldom sickness (i.e. no visitation of the plague) we are grown more populous than ever heretofore.' Add to this the rise in prices beginning around 1500, with a big jump in the 1540s, and the rise in the number of beggars is easily understood. They haunted market place, churchyard and highway. One traveller said of them, 'Ye be affraid to saie naie unto them honestlie lest they take it awaie from you violentlie . . .' At the other end of the social scale, fashionable dress for men as much as for women was complicated, rich and costly in the extreme. Between these two classes the vast majority of Essex people practised their crafts and their trades, serving long apprenticeships while hoping eventually to set up for themselves. Agricultural labourers found no such hope in their employment. There were no important changes in farming techniques through the 16th century. Even for those humble tenants of the lord of the manor who held their lands in the field strips round the village, the age-old, strict three-year rotation of crops, including a year of fallow, was still observed.

Those who travelled through Essex went on horseback or on foot; coaches in the continental fashion were only just being seen on the streets of London. The famous John Leland, who travelled on his 'great tour' for eight years through England and Wales from around 1537, wrote of the 'foul and noyful slough' he encountered on the road from Chelmsford to Stock, and of the main street through Thaxted being 'so gulled with the fall of water that passengers cannot pass.' Country people ploughed through the mud and forded the rivers to get to the 72 centres of trade already set up in this county. Colchester was one of the greatest with the Colne its highway for trade from the estuary up to Halstead, though watermills hindered the passage of all but the smallest craft. In the market, fish from the tidal waters, controlled by the Borough under its charter of 1189, reached the stalls in excellent condition. Colchester oysters became world-famous and the rents of the 'layings' swelled the Borough's coffers.

When religious refugees from the Low Countries crossed the North Sea in the 14th century they brought the secrets and inventions of weaving with them and formed a separate colony in Colchester, echoing the settlement of those superannuated Romans 1,000 years before. They formed a 'staple' – an association of merchants dealing in wool – and

Colchester was declared by royal edict the 'staple town' for the cloth industry in north-east Essex. The importance of this Essex industry was reduced by the depredations of the Civil War and the siege of 1648. Though the weavers and the clothiers struggled on, they could not compete with the centres in the north which, by the early 19th century, had taken over completely.

The state of education from the reign of Henry VIII to Elizabeth I was summed up by Thomas Tusser, the famous agricultural poet born at Rivenhall around 1520. He put his memories of his education at Eton into verse:

'O painful time, for every crime!
What towsed ears, like baited bears!
What bobbed lips, what jerks, what nips!
What hellish toys!
What robes how bare, what college fare!
What bread how stale, what penny ale!

That life for the scholar in Essex was very hard is shown in the written complaint made by Richard Broadway, head of Chelmsford Grammar School, from 1594 to 1608, against his assistant master who, he said, was guilty of 'In the Schoole hearinge the Children negligently, carelessly construinge theire lessons to them ... not trayninge them up in the declininge of nownes, Conjugatinge of verbes nor in writinge as in former times they have bin by others.' Broadway accused him of 'Dispightfully callinge me Jew bidding me kisse his arse, a tord in my teeth and this in the presence and hearing of all the Schollers.' And as to his treatment of the poor boys – 'In the Scholle the dayly whippinge of Richard Younge till he had whipped him forth of the Schoole. Also John Stane driving him out of the Schoole with the blood aboute his eares, breaking his head Twice and severe usinge others as rending piteously the eare of John Sweeting and daily beatinge him.'

Retained by Sir Andrew Paschall to teach his son at home, this man struck the boy so hard on the eye that 'blood gushed forth of his mouth.' He also beat '... a gentleman's daughter that was his Scholler untill all the skin was flayed from her buttocks.' Life was hard for Essex schoolchildren. It was not much better for the youth who had no schooling. He would be bound apprentice to a tradesman or craftsman, would most likely live in his master's house, and for seven long years would be at his beck and call night and day. Books were now being printed in greater numbers, so that self-education of a sort could be achieved. Wynkyn de Worde, Caxton's apprentice, succeeded to that famous first English printer's stock-in-trade in 1491, and one of the books he printed whilst working with Caxton was the first edition of Dame Juliana Berners' extraordinary manuscript on the arts of hunting, hawking, fishing and heraldry. She was the daughter of Sir James Berners, who had been executed in 1388 for remaining loyal to Richard II. His family had held the manor of Rothinges and Berwyk for over a century and gave the settlement its name – Berners Roding.

Juliana grew up in this wild and beautiful river valley and in the woods where game gave sport and food. She went on to the royal court where these sports were so popular. Later she was appointed Prioress of the nunnery at Sopwell in Herts and in the peace of that place she compiled her manuscript, and gave the tiny village a niche in Essex history. Another Essex author who has received little credit for his work is Joseph Strutt. He wrote, drew and engraved all the illustrations for *Sports and Pastimes of the People of England*, first published in 1801. He quotes Burton's *Anatomy of Melancholy* (1660) which gives a good general view of the games played in Essex through the generations:

'Hunting and hawking are honest recreations, and fit for some great men, but not for every base inferior person, who, while they maintain their faulkner, and dogs, and hunting nags, their wealth runs away with their hounds, and their fortunes fly away with their hawks.'

Strutt goes on to list the games which were popular in these swash-buckling days of the Tudors:

'Ringing, bowling, shooting, playing with keel-pins, tronks, coits, pitching of bars, hurling, wrestling, leaping, running, fencing, mustering, swimming, playing with wasters, foils, footballs, balowns, running at the quintain, and the like, are common recreations of country folks.' He considers 'bull-baitings and bear-baitings, in which our citizens greatly delight' and, 'dancers on ropes, jugglers, comedies, tragedies, artillery gardens and cock-fighting' as common in both town and country. Winter pastimes, by the light of the candle, included cards, table dice, shove-ha'penny, billiards, music, dancing and 'merry tales of errant knights, queens, lovers, lords, ladies, giants, dwarfs, thieves, witches, fairies and so on.'

It would seem that Essex Elizabethans filled what little time they had for recreation with a wide variety of imaginative self-amusement.

Football in Essex was already claiming casualties. On 10th March 1567 when a match was played in Branton Mead, Hatfield Broad Oak, Henry Ingold of White Roding collided with Thomas Paviott in a challenge for the ball. Henry did not get up again. By midnight he was dead. In 1582

John Pye, keeping goal for Gosfield men against Bocking, was knocked down by Richard Elye and later died. So did John Warde in a match between East and West Ham in the same year. An even greater tragedy occurred when the village lads were larking about in the millpond at St Osyth in 1576. One youth had procured two pig's bladders and tied them round his body as water wings. They leaked, he began to sink and shouted out, 'I'm drowning, for the love of God save me!' Two boys stretched out their hands to pull him to the side, their feet slipped, they fell in and all three were drowned.

One recreation then enjoyed by people of all ages was the theatre. It had its roots deeply set in the church 'miracle plays' which told the stories of the Bible, of creation and of man's journey through life to heaven or hell, according to his merits. From these tableaux with their moral tales developed the secular drama of Shakespeare. One of the centres for such plays was Chelmsford. Even today the Cathedral, formerly the humble parish church, preserves a unique feature of those days. In the great stone piers which take the weight of the tower there are two huge cupboards; these are where all the props were stored for the miracle plays which made Chelmsford an important centre of 16th century drama. They are the largest lockers of this kind to be found anywhere in England.

It is still possible to read the accounts kept by the churchwardens of materials bought, work done and income received from hiring out costumes belonging to Chelmsford church. In 1564, for example we read, 'Recayved of Coulchester men for our garments for the use of there playe – 43s. 3d.' In that year alone the costumes were borrowed by Saffron Walden, Billericay, Baddow and Bishop's Stortford. In 1562 the Chelmsford actors took their play and costumes to Braintree. It is strange to think that one essential in an actor's repertory then was the ability to ride a horse. They took their play to Maldon as well. Both performances show the importance of the Chelmsford plays, for these two towns had players of their own. It is a pity that no text of their plays has survived.

In 1573 an inventory of all the costume and props was made, and the following year there appeared in the accounts: '. . . soulde unto George Studlye and others, all the ropes, vestments,. . . players coats, jerkens, gownes, heares, cappes, berds, jornetts, mantells and capes mentioned in the Inventorye of the last Churchwardens . . .' The ending of church plays was in sight and the citizens at large, increasingly puritanical, showed their displeasure at these gaudy goings-on by breaking the church windows of beautiful stained glass. That was in 1576, and the plays stopped abruptly.

The changing of religious attitudes by successive rulers throughout the 16th century, from Henry VIII through the reigns of Edward VI, Queen Mary and Queen Elizabeth, brought sad and shameful times for Essex. The newly formed English nation began slowly to turn away from the age-old belief introduced to the Saxons and confirmed with enthusiasm by the Normans. The pomp and circumstance of the Roman form of Christianity contrasted with the hardships of ordinary Essex people's daily life. The veiling of the holy books, written in Latin, from the eyes and understanding of common folk, was another cause of dissension. Pilgrimages to sacred places in Essex had taken on a thoroughly commercial air. When Henry VIII came to the throne there was a strong movement against corruption within the Church, fostered in Essex by the so-called 'heretics' fleeing from the Low Countries into Colchester and northern Essex to escape persecution, torture and death.

The priors and abbots of religious foundations had long been envied for their self-indulgent, lazy way of life. It was Parliament as much as Henry, the Head of the Church, which brought about the Reformation. In 1524 the closure of the smallest monasteries began, and gathered momentum after Wolsey's fall from grace in 1529. The Abbot of St John's Abbey, Colchester, John Beche, was present at the Parliament of 1539 when the Act of conveyance of monastery property to the crown was passed. He publicly declared 'The King shall never have my house but against my will and against my heart . . .' According to local tradition, 'The magistrates asked him to a feast and then showed him the warrant and went and hanged him without further warning or ceremony, on December 1st, 1539.' By 1540 the Reformation was complete.

It was Henry's quarrel with Pope Clement VII, in his attempt to get his marriage with Catherine of Aragon dissolved that brought the final break with Rome. Ordinary Essex men and women were little affected by this change. They saw their local monastery or nunnery taken over by some wealthy, time-serving courtier or knocked down out of hand. Where they had used part of the building as their parish church, the king granted permission for its retention. Examples of pre-Reformation buildings which have survived can be seen at Hatfield Peverel (Priory), Tilty (Abbey), Little Dunmow (Priory), which sponsored the famous Dunmow Flitch trials of wedded bliss, at Barking (Abbey) and in other Essex parishes. Considerable hostility was shown in Essex against the parish priests of the day, who had grown lax and uncaring. The holding of many benefices by one rich priest who put in underlings as curates on starvation wages, a system known as 'pluralism', was very common. The fundamentalist teaching of Luther had been brought across the sea by refugee weavers who settled over a wide region of north Essex. They had already suffered persecution in Essex for their faith; over a hundred of them were arrested for heresy before Henry VIII's battle with Rome diverted attention from them.

Under Edward VI when clerical marriage was first allowed, and again under Elizabeth, war was declared on the rich and gaudy decoration of the old Church. Images of saints, altar pieces, stained glass windows and wall paintings were all attacked. The paintings were whitewashed and replaced with printed texts. It can truly be said that the Reformation struck a blow at the beauty of worship. Between these two reigns there was a revival of Catholic splendour when Mary ruled from 1553 for just five years. She brought back the old religion but the furious persecution of Protestants, instituted by her specially appointed Archbishop of Canterbury, Reginald Pole, earned her the sobriquet 'Bloody Mary'. Of the 300 or so 'heretics' tortured and then killed and burned at the stake, 73 came from Essex.

George Eagles was a tailor. A wandering tailor, because George's faith came before his work, and he trudged from place to place preaching the Protestant faith. He became well-known in the market places of Essex, gaining the nickname 'Trudge-over-the-world Eagles', affectionately shortened to 'Trudgeover'. His persistence came to the ears of the Queen's advisers. A royal proclamation sent out through Essex and three counties bordering it, offered a reward of £20 for information leading to his capture. One market day he preached at Colchester to an admiring crowd, but was recognised by the authorities and had to run for his life out of town. He hid in the middle of a cornfield. One of his pursuers saw the corn sway as Trudgeover wriggled away and sounded the alarm. He was caught and that informer got his reward.

George Eagles was taken to London, examined, and sentenced to death. He was brought back to the Crown Inn at Chelmsford, which then served as the county prison. Then he was brought out, tied to a hurdle and dragged down the High Street by a horse to the Stone Bridge, where a gibbet had been set up. There he was hanged, but the rope did not strangle him. It was cut as he struggled and he fell to the ground. He was then dragged to the hurdle and his head was propped up on it whilst a man took an ordinary kitchen chopper from a house nearby. With this he struck at poor Trudgeover's head repeatedly without severing it cleanly, killing the man cruelly in cold blood. His head was stuck on a spike on the market cross and his body, disembowelled, was cut in quarters, each part to be displayed in a different market place in the county, as a warning to others.

Thomas Haukes of Coggeshall was not an upstart or a rabble-rouser. He was the son of a gentleman and was employed in the service of the Earl of Oxford in the time of Edward VI. When Queen Mary re-introduced the Roman Catholic form of Christianity the Earl of Oxford found it expedient to follow the royal faith, but Thomas Haukes stayed faithful to the old beliefs, left the court and returned to quiet home life with his wife and their new baby. But he made the fateful decision to delay the baby's baptism – a sure sign of his Protestant belief – and people who were once his friends denounced him to his old master. The Earl did not want to get embroiled in this religious controversy so he sent Thomas on to the wicked Bonner, Bishop of London, accompanied by a guard with a letter stating the case.

Bonner challenged Thomas straight away by asking why he had left his child unbaptised for so long. Over days of intensive questioning Thomas stuck fast to his faith, so his fate was sealed. On 10th June, 1555, he was sent in Lord Rich's custody to Coggeshall, where he was chained to a stake on top of a heap of faggots. A flaming brand was shoved into the pyre, and a very brave man died agonisingly for his faith. William Hunter, the 19 year old Brentwood martyr, went to the stake in the same year. His story is told in Foxe's *Book of Martyrs*.

Elizabeth's accession in 1558 brought relief to Protestants. She followed a middle way. Everybody was required to attend church regularly under pain of a shilling fine. Extremists in both directions were held to be guilty of treason for challenging the declared belief of the Queen herself. There were still some rotten apples in the barrel of the reformed religion. The *Register* of parish clergy compiled at this time lists a Mr Goldring, parson of Langdon Hills as being convicted of fornication and being a drunkard; and 'Mr Durden, parson of Mashbury, a careless man, a gamester, an alehouse haunter, a company keeper with drunkards, and he himself sometimes drunk.'

As religious persecution was the terror of Mary's reign, so witchcraft was of Elizabeth's, and Essex was very much involved. An Act against the practice of witchcraft had been passed in Henry VIII's reign. In 1563 a further Act was passed which distinguished between different kinds of sorcery. For all attempts to conjure up evil spirits and for murder by witchcraft the penalty was death, by hanging or burning. In lesser cases the penalty for a first offence was a year's imprisonment; subsequent offences brought life imprisonment or death. James I was so convinced of the reality of witchcraft that he wrote a book on the subject, called *Daemonology*, published in 1597, and he introduced a harsher law in 1604. He believed in the proof of guilt obtained by 'swimming' a witch, a superstition which persisted in Essex right down to the 19th century.

Although it was the Roman church which first persecuted heretics as so-called witches, under Elizabeth and James it was the turn of extreme protestants to use the accusation of witchcraft for their own ends. Bishop Jewel reported to Queen Elizabeth, '. . . witches and sorcerers have marvellously increased within your Grace's realm. Your Grace's subjects pine away unto death. Their colour fadeth, their flesh rotteth, their speech is benumbed, their senses are bereft.' Witches were supposed to have 'imps' or 'familiars', devils who carried out their wicked commands. These creatures could be of all shapes and sizes and were said to be suckled in some mysterious manner by the witches themselves.

A major trial of witches took place at the Assize held in Chelmsford in 1566. A transcript of the proceedings still exists. One of the accused, Elizabeth Francis of Hatfield Peverel, is said to have learned the art of witchcraft when she was twelve, from her grandmother Eve. 'When she taught it her, she counselled her to renounce God and his word and to give of her blood to Satan (as she termed it) which she delivered her in the likeness of a white spotted cat . . . also she taught her to call it by the name of Satan and to keep it in a basket.' When her husband and child died she was accused of bewitching them.

In 1582 no fewer than 13 women from the Tendring area were put on trial at Chelmsford. Elizabeth Byett was hanged. So was Ursula Kemp, who said that she had once consulted with a witch because of her lameness. She was given the following recipe: Dog's dung mixed with charnel must be pricked with a knife three times and then thrown into the fire. The knife must be stuck three times into the table and left sticking there. Then she was to drink sage and herb grace in her ale and her health would improve. It worked so well that Ursula set up on her own account, issuing that one recipe to all sufferers, whatever their ailment. Her own illegitimate child of eight years old was put forward as a witness against her. She was hanged. Her skeleton, buried in unconsecrated ground, was discovered under the floor of a cottage in Mill Street, St Osyth, around 1921. From then until the cottage was destroyed by fire in 1931 these sad remains were put on exhibition. People paid a fee, a trapdoor was opened, and there were the pathetic remains of Ursula Kemp, with iron spikes pinning the body down through hips, elbows and knees. The Elizabethans believed that this would prevent a witch's resurrection.

In 1589 four out of nine women and one man put on trial were hanged. They had all been brought down to Chelmsford from Elmstead and Great Oakley. In the Boreham parish burial register for 1593 there is the entry 'Mother Haven suffered at Boreham for witchcraft.' It says much for the persistence of superstition in Essex that, when the

This grand house, Ingatestone Hall, was the last word in modern building when Queen Elizabeth stayed here as the guest of Sir William Petre in 1561.

Americans were building Boreham airfield in the Second World War and dug up human bones, villagers declared that a disease among cattle at that time could be put down to the witch's anger at the disturbance of her grave!

The Elizabethan working man led a very hard life. Infant mortality was high and whole communities were carried off by frightful plagues. Their attitude to death was pragmatic – it happened so frequently. That is why public hangings became as much a spectacle as the baiting of a bull or bear.

The connection between Elizabeth I and Essex was emphasised by the various 'Progresses' she made through the eastern counties. Take, for example the tours she made of Essex over the period 1561 to 1588, visiting 24 of the houses of courtiers and gentry who lived in Essex. In July 1561 she set out for her own royal palace at Havering-atte-Bower. In a couple of days she moved on to Wanstead House where she was received by the Earl of Leicester. Then it was on to Loughton Hall,

John Stonard's house. By the end of July she had spent a few days at Ingatestone Hall with Sir William Petre, when his house, built in 1540, was still a wonder of the age. After a short stay at New Hall, Boreham, a royal palace built for Henry VIII, the Queen and her large entourage went on to Felix Hall at Kelvedon where they were entertained by the Cecils. (The present house was not built until 1760 or thereabouts.) On 26th July, Elizabeth, with typical vigour, rallied her retainers and set forth for St John's Abbey, Colchester, the mansion of the Lucas family. At the end of the month she was safely ensconced in Lord Darcy's palatial residence in the former St Osyth's Priory, granted to him in 1553 and converted in the grand manner. Gosfield Hall was the next stop. It had been built by Sir John Wentworth and was then occupied by his daughter, Lady Mautravers.

By 21st August the 'progress' was on its return journey via Leez Priory at Little Leighs, home of Lord Rich, former Chancellor and his son Robert, 2nd Lord Rich, who had been created a Knight of the Bath at Elizabeth's coronation. The actual Priory had been demolished in order to raise their new, prestigious house with its impressive gatehouse. The royal party left on 25th August and arrived on the same day at Hallingbury Place on the other side of the county, owned by Henry, 11th Lord Morley. In September the Queen's host was the 16th Earl of Oxford at Hedingham Castle. Less than 40 years later all but the stone keep of that castle had been destroyed.

Three progresses through Essex in the 1570s included other great houses. Evidence of the vibrant life of these times under a vital, able Queen is shown in the fact that most of these substantial homes were built during her reign. Some of the owners, like Sir Thomas Mildmay, rather rued the expense involved in providing food and entertainment for the large retinue. He had to dip deep into his pocket when Moulsham Hall was selected for the honour of Her Majesty's presence in September 1579. The shortest and most important 'progress' Queen Elizabeth made was in 1588 when she stayed at Arden Hall, Horndon-on-the-Hill, home of Thomas Rich, on the way to the Camp Royal at Tilbury where an army was being assembled to resist

Tilbury Fort, where Queen Elizabeth I made her stirring Armada speech in 1588, to the assembled army. The fort is now in the care of English Heritage.

the threat of the Spanish Armada. Here she addressed her troops with the famous words: '. . . I am come amongst you, as you see, at this time, not for my recreation or disport, but being resolved, in the midst and heat of the battle, to live and die amongst you all, to lay down for my God, for my kingdom and for my people, my honour and my blood, even in the dust. I know I have but the body of a weak and feeble woman, but I have the heart and stomach of a king, and a King of England too . . .'

We cannot close this chapter without reference to a man who lived in Essex for 34 years and is described by a modern scholar in these words: 'Too limited to rise above his age, he mirrors it almost perfectly. He not only describes the Elizabethan scene, he thinks and speaks as an ordinary Elizabethan. In Harrison we come exceptionally close to that elusive aspect in the study of the past, what the common people thought about common things.' These are the closing words of Georges Edeben's Introduction to William Harrison's, *The Description of England*, published in 1577 with a second edition in 1587.

William Harrison was Rector of Radwinter for 34 years until his death in 1593. In that rectory he wrote this amazing work on all aspects of the life of his age; so detailed, so vigorous, so enthusiastic – typically Elizabethan. 'I would wish that I might live no longer than to see four things in this land reformed, that is: the want of discipline in the church; the covetous dealings of most of our merchants in the preferment of the commodities of other countries and the hindrance of their own; the holding of fairs and markets upon the Sunday to be abolished and referred to Wednesdays; and that every man in whatsoever part of the champaign [country] who enjoyeth forty acres of land and upwards, after that rate, either by free deed, copyhold, or fee farm, might plant one acre of wood with oak mast, hazel, beech, and sufficient provision be made and kept. But I fear me that I should then live too long . . .'

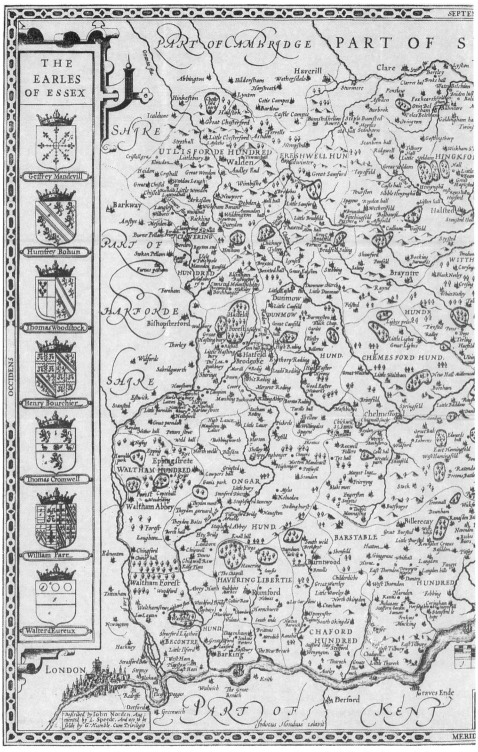

John Speede's decorated map of 1610 showing the county at the end of the Tudor period.

9

THE STUARTS, CIVIL WAR AND COMMONWEALTH

The rule of the Stuart kings until the Civil War has been described by G M Trevelyan in *English Social History* as '. . . an uneventful prolongation of the Elizabethan era, under conditions of peace and safety instead of domestic danger and foreign war.' We should not, however, forget the Gunpowder Plot of 5th November 1605, which could have had appalling effects. But let us begin at the beginning. When James I passed through Waltham on his way to enthronement in London he was welcomed by Sir Edward Denny, High Sheriff of Essex, who had assembled 140 of his men, specially kitted out in blue and white uniforms and mounted on horses with bright red saddles. So the new King had an early acquaintance with the loyal inhabitants of Essex, and by 1626 Sir Edward Denny got his reward – advancement from a peerage in 1604 to the dignity of the Earldom of Norwich in 1626.

The King saw more of the people of west Essex as he spent a lot of time hunting through the forests around Epping and Waltham and enjoying the hospitality of courtiers with country houses in the area. After the hunt there was considerable gaiety. Arthur Wilson, gentleman-in-waiting to Robert Devereux, 3rd Earl of Essex, a keen observer and writer on the life of these times, recorded that the Scotsmen who came down with James '. . . not only crept into English lordships but also into the beds of English ladies.'

Many of those honours bestowed by James were a straightforward exchange for services rendered or for money loaned. Thus were members of the hunting fraternity rewarded. Francis Barrington of Hatfield Broad Oak, who married the daughter of Oliver Cromwell's grandfather, was knighted at the forest mansion of Theobalds in 1603 and advanced to a baronetcy as soon as that order was introduced by James in 1611. Henry Maynard of Little Easton, first of the family to settle in Essex, where he built Easton Lodge, represented the county in Parliament. James knighted him in 1603 and elevated his son William as 1st Baron Maynard of Estaines Parva (Little Easton) in 1628. Sir John

Petre became Baron Petre of Writtle in 1603, having been knighted by Elizabeth in 1575.

The Barringtons had lived for generations at Hatfield Broad Oak. There is a letter still in existence from Mr Francis Barrington's tailor advising him on how to dress for his first royal audience with James:

> '. . . in black, without all cuttings . . . I have inquired concerning cloaks and can hear of but one rich cloak which is worn, but the most part be of black velvet or grogram or cloth.'

Dress was certainly not as sumptuous and fantastic as it had been in Elizabeth's day. James's queen, Anne, who was too ill to travel from Scotland at the time of his accession, came south later and was greeted at the border by a goodly number of ladies of the English aristocracy in a demonstration of loyalty. One of them was Penelope, Lady Rich, daughter of Walter Devereux, 1st Earl of Essex. A high-spirited lady, popular with Queen Elizabeth, she had parted from her husband, Lord Rich, later created 1st Earl of Warwick, not long after their marriage in 1580. She was the 'Stella' of sonnets by Sir Philip Sidney (1554–86). When he died she transferred her affections to Lord Mountjoy, 8th Baron Blount, created Earl of Devonshire by James in 1603. The new queen liked her enough to make her a Lady of the Bedchamber. When Lord Rich did at last divorce her, in 1605, she was able to marry Mountjoy. The Archbishop Laud, then starting on the ladder of fame, was Mountjoy's private chaplain. He performed the ceremony reluctantly, because the marriage of a divorcee was against the law of the church. It lay so heavily on his conscience in later years that he always fasted on that particular day. As lovers they had been acceptable at court. Married illegally they were not. Shunned by all, they were both dead before the following year was out. Wanstead House saw their celebration, their degradation and decline.

It was to an Essex man, William Parker, Lord Monteagle of Great Hallingbury Hall, that the letter was sent which led to the discovery of the plot to blow up Parliament with 36 barrels of gunpowder on 5th November 1605. The letter advised '. . . I have a care of your preservation, therefore would advise you, as you tender your life, to devise some excuse to shift off your attendance at the Parliament . . . retire yourself into your county, where you may expect the event in safety . . . they will receive a terrible blow this Parliament, and yet they will not see who hurts them . . .' Lord Monteagle did not fly in fear; he led a party to the vaults of Parliament, and organised the watch which led to the apprehension of the plotters that night. He was rewarded with a pension of £700 a year for his loyalty and his bravery. At this time the county was represented in Parliament by two 'Knights of the Shire' – first called to conference with the king in 1290 and actually elected to that position by qualified freeholders from 1430 – together with two members of Parliament chosen for each of the chartered boroughs of Colchester, Harwich and Maldon. The elections were held in Chelmsford, the county town, where the population was swelled by the voters crowding in from all over the county.

James I was constantly short of money. He sold honours to his courtiers, but the gentry of Essex did not look with favour on his call in 1604 for a loan unapproved by Parliament. Amongst these sturdily independent men were Samuel Ailine, Paul Bayning, Henry Baker of North Shoebury, John Barefoot of Lambourne, Edward Grimston, Sir Thomas Knightley, Humphrey Mildmay, Roger Gittens of South Weald and William Kemp of Finchingfield. They were not so foolish as to question the legality of the loan, but said they could not raise the sum required of them.

It was William Kemp who started a delightful folk-tale still related around his old home at Finchingfield. He was born at Spains Hall in 1555. In 1621, in a jealous rage, he accused his wife of being unfaithful. Then, realising how wrong he had been, he vowed not to utter another word for seven years, as a self-inflicted penance. Even after his wife died in 1623 he persisted in this terrible self-punishment. He marked the passing of each year by the excavation of a fish pond in his garden. It was said by Sir William Addison that, at the end of those seven years Kemp became so agitated that he more or less collapsed, and when he tried to call for help he could not utter a sound. The shock killed him. The long inscription on his tomb in Finchingfield church tells the story:

> 'Here lies William Kemp, Esq., pious, just, hospitable, master of himself so much that what others scarce do by force and penalties, he did by a voluntary constancy hold his peace for seven years . . .'

His 400 year old house of red brick, stone dressing and curious Dutch gables still stands, and south-east of it is a lake, an amalgamation of two of those fish ponds he commissioned without a word being uttered.

Another great house connected with James himself is Audley End, built to the order of Thomas Howard, 1st Earl of Suffolk (1561–1626). He had married Margaret Audley, daughter of the Lord Chancellor. It was 13 years in the building, from 1603. So much of it has been pulled down since, that its true glory can hardly be appreciated. The Earl and his Countess stooped to every device to bring the great work to completion. When King James went to visit it, shortly after he had appointed Howard to the office of Lord Treasurer, he was so amazed by the scale of the

Built in 1605 to the order of Thomas Howard, First Earl of Suffolk, Audley End took 13 years to build. This engraving is by Henry Winstanley, Clerk of Works in the building of Audley End, and is part of a series of 24 engravings of his plans. What we see today (below) is only about half the original, after a process of demolition and renovation. The gardens and grounds were designed by Robert Adam and 'Capability' Brown.

building that he quipped, 'By my troth, man, it is too much for a king, but may do for a Lord High Treasurer!' Within two years, suspicion of bribery and corruption in their great building scheme brought the Earl and his wife before the Star Chamber court and commitment to the Tower for ten days. The Earl lost all his offices and was fined £30,000. He lived for another six years, then died at the Great House, as he called it, which he no longer could afford to keep in repair. Now it is in the hands of the Department of the Environment and open to the public.

The Catholics incurred the King's hostility through the Gunpowder Plot; but the rise of Puritan ideas for the reform of the English Church was equally unwelcome. Their habit of simple worship without the show of rich vestments, 'graven images' and precious metals for ornaments was winning converts who, largely unlettered, were much influenced by the powerful preaching which was such a feature of the new ministry. Take, for instance, the happening in Chelmsford on 5th November 1641, when the Gunpowder Plot was still within the memory of older inhabitants. A mob of Puritans, nonconformists, aroused by a ranting local leader telling of Parliament's edict that all 'scandalous' pictures should be removed from churches, advanced on the churchyard of St Mary's (now the Cathedral) with stones in their pockets to smash the beautiful coloured glass of the big east window. It was more than 200 years old, dating from the restoration of the church in 1424, and depicted in glowing colours the life of Christ, with coats of arms of the generous benefactors. The churchwardens had already removed the frames depicting the Virgin Mary and the Crucifixion, but that was not enough for the excited mob.

The Rector, Dr Michaelson, was abused and threatened with physical harm. Two weeks later a dissenter attacked him in church and tried to tear off his surplice because in the Puritan mind this simple garment was part of the panoply of Roman worship. The worthy Doctor was forced out of his living and he and his family, including eight children, had to live on the charity of friends in nearby Writtle until he was restored to his position and possessions upon the Restoration of Charles II. The leader of the 'anabaptists' in Chelmsford at the time of the riots was a man who called himself 'Parson Oates', father of the conspirator Titus Oates (1649–1705).

Such antipathy towards the established church was demonstrated all over Essex. In 1640 soldiers encamped at Radwinter tramped unceremoniously into the church (another St Mary's) and smashed down a recently erected screen between chancel and nave. It was of wood, beautifully carved with cherubim floating from on high. They took all those figures in a waggon to Saffron Walden, and burned them in the market place as a protest against the separation of the priest from the congregation. According to an eye-witness:

> 'William Voyle, pretending authority to be the lecturer of the aforesaid parish . . . coming into the church in the time of divine service with a great cudgel in his hand, came directly to the reading desk where the aforesaid Richard Drake was performing his duty; and in a violent manner . . . laid both his hands upon the said Richard Drake, endeavouring to thrust him out of the desk . . .'

Drake was knocked down but got up again and clutched the pulpit door, only to be felled again by Voyle and four others who dragged him the length of the church on his back, and threw him out of the door. If the congregation had not come to his rescue, they would have murdered him.

In 1642 an enraged crowd gathered outside the rectory at Ardleigh, shouted obscenities, broke down the door and looted everything of any value. The rector was chased down the road in a hail of mud and stones. The only place where he could escape their violence was in the village 'cage', the tiny temporary village jail. When one stands in the beautiful St Mary's church at Thaxted, enjoying peace of the place, it is hard to imagine the cursing and swearing, the struggling and fighting which went on there on Friday, 24th September, 1647. The vicar, Newman Leader, had been replaced by the more puritan Mr Hall, the people's choice; but Lady Maynard should have been consulted, for she had the power of appointment of the vicar of this parish. A very independent lady, she chose Edmund Croxon, even though he had a reputation as a drunken blackguard. She would not give in, so a great crowd of Thaxted parishioners gathered to escort their man Mr Hall to the church to preach the sermon. When they tried again in the afternoon the churchwardens barred his way to the pulpit, on Lady Maynard's instructions. The crowd become violent, grabbed the church officials, beat them and it is said, 'tore out their hair in handfuls', making them flee for their lives. The ringleaders were apprehended and taken for trial before the House of Lords that same day, proof of the importance the government attached to this continuing religious unrest in Essex. A London bookseller had a pamphlet printed on the '. . . Great Fight in the Church at Thaxted.'

From the beginning of the 17th century, when the Puritans saw that they could not effect the reforms they wanted within the Church, they formed their own separate circles of worshippers, meeting in each other's houses. But they were prosecuted so relentlessly that many in Essex emigrated to the New World, to practice their faith in total freedom.

Robert Rich, 2nd Earl of Warwick, whose family home was Leez priory, had been Member of Parliament for Maldon before succeeding his father as Earl in 1619. He was a great adventurer in the Puritan cause, helping to set up the colonies of New Plymouth, Massachusetts, Connecticut and Rhode Island. He returned to Essex to lead the Puritan faction, raising an army to support the cause of Parliament in the Civil War. Eventually, in 1643, he was appointed Lord High Admiral of the Fleet, much to his pleasure, for he was a sailor through and through. He was also appointed head of the Commission for the government of the colonies in 1643. 'Warwick, with all his faults,' says Sir William Addison, 'was one of the greatest men the county has known.' Others included in this great American adventure included John Winthrop, first Governor of Massachusetts, who lived at Great Stambridge after marrying a local heiress, Mary Forth. She died when he was only 28; within 18 months he was married and widowed again. His third wife shared both the hardship and happiness when he settled finally at Charlestown and was elected Governor of Massachusetts in 1631.

Christopher Martin, a Billericay miller, was treasurer to another expedition of Puritans to the New World. They arrived off the American coast in 1620 during a terrible winter and most of the emigrants died of disease on board before they could put a foot ashore. Christopher Martin was one of them.

Meanwhile, back in England, King James died on 27th March, 1625, at his favourite palace, Theobalds. His son succeeded him as Charles I, a ruler whose machinations greatly affected Essex. He needed money, and would get it without Parliament's approval if necessary. He summoned and dissolved Parliament no less than three times in the first four years of his reign, then for eleven years ruled without it, using subservient judges and the fearful courts of Star Chamber and High Commission.

In that same year of 1625 the Chelmsford Churchwardens' accounts shed a strange sidelight on Essex. They show that the terrible plague rampaging through London and Essex at that time resulted in great expenditure by the church – on wine. It happened in this way: once the plague manifested itself in the filthy alleys of the London slums, the gentry and merchants headed out of the city for the healthier air of Essex and further north. Chelmsford was the stopping place for the first night. With their families and servants they increased the risk of plague being spread as they crowded into the close confines of the town's inns. As it spread, the townsfolk and the refugees were so desperate that, Puritan or no, they trooped into the church to pray for deliverance and took the bread and wine of holy communion. In an ordinary year the churchwardens reckoned to spend 38 shillings on bread and wine. In

1625 the record shows that they had to find £8, more than four times the usual cost. The plague passed on north with the fleeing Londoners. When it came again to Colchester in 1665–6, 4,731 inhabitants died from it, according to D W Coller.

In the first summer of Charles I's reign, Spain was assembling a fleet of ships at Dunkirk, so it was thought prudent to improve the defences of Harwich and Colchester, which were most likely to be attacked. In the autumn that fleet was seen sailing off Harwich, causing William Lynne of Bradfield Hall to call on Colchester for help because Harwich, he said, was 'weakly provided to defend itself, and the countrie soldiers destitute of powder, bullets, and many other necessaries ...' Fortunately it was a false alarm – the Spaniards sailed on by. The dissatisfaction in the army with the lack of preparedness, and the lack of cash to improve it, was reflected in a minor mutiny when the King attempted to raise a military force to be transported across the north sea to support the King of Denmark in 1627. Just a few months later a tax was levied on the county to kit out and transport 150 impressed Essex men coerced to join an expedition against France at the whim of the King.

These were minor irritations. As Sir William Addison wrote, 'Most of the troubles of the 17th century had their roots in religion. What are thought of as parsons' quarrels now were people's quarrels then. Politics hung upon theology, and theology seems to have been the most vital thing in life after the permanent biological interests had been provided for.' In 1634 there was further resistance from Essex and Suffolk to the King's demand for 'Ship Money' from the Boroughs of Harwich, Colchester and Maldon; a tax which they were to collect from their inhabitants towards the building and fitting out of a 700-ton warship at a projected cost of £6,615. It was but a ghost-ship, the King's excuse for raising another large contribution to his dwindling coffers. Another £8,000 was demanded from the county in the following year. The King was attacking the people of Essex where it hurt them most – in their pockets.

Yet the religious persecution went on. A last example of the determination of the King, as head of the Church, to stamp out Puritanism was the case of John Bastwick. He was born in Writtle in 1593, educated at Emmanuel College, Cambridge, wandered around Europe for nine years, took a degree in medicine at Padua, and came back to Colchester to practice. In pamphlets printed in Holland from 1633 he expressed his belief in the new simple way of worship, attacking the flagrant abuses of their trust by the bishops and priests of the established church. His authorship proved, he was taken before the infamous Star Chamber court which handled cases concerning such offences for which the existing law made no provision. He was fined £1,000, excommunicated and sent to prison until he withdrew those written accusations. He was 'struck off' as we would say today and all copies of his books were ordered to be burnt.

Bastwick was made of stern stuff. He did not recant; instead he wrote more tracts while he was in prison, inveighing against the tyranny of the court which had wrongly imprisoned him. That court punished him further; he was put in the pillory. Then it was ordered that both his ears should be cut off and he was sentenced to perpetual imprisonment in the most distant jail in the country, at that time on the Scilly Isles. Even in the courtroom John Bastwick stood up to his persecutors, crying out, 'What, will you cut off a true and loyal subject's ears for doing his duty to his king and country? Will you cut off a scholar's ears? Will you cut off a doctor of physic's ears, able to cure lords, peers, kings and

John Bastwick suffered terribly for his faith under Charles I's determination to stamp out Puritanism. After being fined, excommunicated, imprisoned, pilloried and mutilated, Bastwick was eventually able to go free and in 1640 Parliament awarded him £5,000 in compensation from the estates of the Church.

emperors? Will you cut off a christian's ears?. . . what an age we live in, that we must thus be exposed to the merciless fury of every malignant spirit!' To no avail. His ears were hacked off and he was sent to his island jail.

The story did have a happy ending, though the poor doctor had to endure seven years' imprisonment until, in 1640, Parliament, now in the ascendant, had that vicious court verdict set aside and awarded Bastwick compensation of £5,000 from the estates of the Church. It was not until 1644 that he actually received enough of that sum to be able to maintain his wife and himself. It must have been an exciting moment when the carriage bringing him back reached London, for there a great crowd turned out to welcome him in triumphal fashion, waving green boughs and casting flowers before him.

The church, becoming increasingly Protestant, turned many an Essex parson out of his living, regardless of the distress and poverty it caused them and their families. Lawrence Washington, the great-great-grandfather of George Washington, was ejected from Purleigh rectory on the grounds that he was '. . . a common frequenter of alehouses, not only himself sitting daily tippling there, but also encouraging others in the beastly vice.' The fact that Washington had royalist leanings was not mentioned.

Most royalist sympathy came from places well away from the wicked influence of London; places where the spicy contents of the bubbling cauldron of Elizabethan court life and trading entrepreneurism had never been tasted. Essex, running as it did up to the very gates of the City of London, had tasted that heady diet of greater freedom of worship, of opportunities in trade and politics and of a steadily advancing system of rule by a Parliament which by the standards of the day could be said to have been democratically elected. So it threw in its lot with the 'Roundheads' by joining the Eastern Association, which had been set up in 1642 to represent the interests of Essex, Suffolk, Norfolk, Cambridgeshire, Hertfordshire and the Isle of Ely. Essex members of this Parliamentary committee included Sir Thomas Barrington, Sir Richard Everard, Sir Harbottle Grimston, Sir Thomas Honeywood, Sir William Masham, Sir Henry Mildmay, Sir Martin Lumley, Henry Holcroft, William Martin and Joseph Sayer. Membership changed between 1642 and 1645 and in 1655.

It appointed a committee to raise large sums of money on a weekly basis for the maintenance of the armed forces under Parliamentary command, by an assessment upon each county. The Essex Committee called on 1,919 gentlemen for contributions. Those who would not pay had their estates sequestered, retaining a fifth which provided a means of maintenance of their families. Later they were allowed to recover that property on the payment of huge fines. Over 50 important estates were thus recovered. The largest sum paid as a contribution was £4,706 by the Right Hon Lord Capel, but the Lucases, well-known royalists, had to find £4,779 among the three of them. They suffered grievously for their loyalty to the King. Sir John 'experienced the ungovernable insolence of a licentious band'. Sir Charles lost his life.

As the Civil War loomed, religious stances were taken up. The Anglican or High Church group in the established church, under Archbishop William Laud, a former rector of West Tilbury, supported the King. The Puritans favoured Parliament, including among their number famous preachers like Stephen Marshall, vicar of Finchingfield. When the rift between King and Commons widened, Sir Thomas Barrington headed the committee for the administration of the county set up by Parliament upon the outbreak of hostilities in 1642. He worked tirelessly to integrate Essex in the war effort, until his untimely death in 1644. The ancient system of county government through the Quarter Sessions and the Justices of the Peace was suspended in 1643, but all matters of county administration were dealt with in that year by Sir Thomas and his fellow justices, so the situation was what we might call today, 'the same difference.'

In the Civil War from 1642 to 1646 most Essex men rallied to Parliament behind their leaders, the Earl of Warwick and Sir Thomas Barrington. The Lucases, Lord Petre and Lord Maynard clung to the royalist cause. Cromwell's New Model Army eventually won that war. To provide for it the county had to supply on a monthly basis payments of cash far in excess of the hated Ship Money, but in this cause they were happy so to do. In August 1642 news had reached Colchester that the Royal Standard had been raised at Nottingham, which was the signal for ordinary Essex folk to go on the attack. One of the few outspoken royalists in Colchester was Sir John Lucas. In his house and grounds he had gathered some 200 armed horsemen – 'Cavaliers'. He judged this was the time to take his little army to join the King's troops. He thought it wisest to leave by the back entrance to his park, but Captain John Langley, grocer, leader of the Colchester trained band, had anticipated this. He led his soldiers at the head of some 2,000 anti-royalist working men from the town and from as far away as Coggeshall, Braintree, Bocking and Halstead, who caught the Cavaliers and forced them to surrender. They had already taken the parson of Holy Trinity prisoner and threw him into jail along with some members of the Lucas family. Then the mob took over, looting the house of all its contents. They even broke into the Lucas family vaults at St Giles and smashed open the coffins to fling about the remains of long dead Lucas ancestors. Sir John Lucas and the parson were taken the next day to London, in Sir Thomas Barrington's own coach, accompanied by his friend Sir Harbottle Grimston. The news of this first incident in the war in Essex spread so rapidly that as they passed along the highway through Chelmsford and Romford people poured out of their houses to cheer them on their way. The Colchester mob went on its avenging way to Long Melford where they robbed and wrecked the house of Lady Rivers, a Roman Catholic and royalist of wide repute.

On 18th July 1642 a number of Essex gentlemen signed a declaration of loyalty to the King, in the hope that he would recall Parliament and take note of the wishes of the people at large. Sir Thomas Bendish of Steeple Bumpstead was behind this 'Grand Remonstrance' designed to reconcile King and Parliament. This resulted in two years' imprisonment in the Tower of London and the sequestration of his estates. On his release he still tried to be a loyal servant of his country as demonstrated by this little bit of folklore: in 1647 he was sent from Essex to be Ambassador at the court of the Grand Vizier of Turkey, a man who was determined to show that he was not impressed by Britain's reputation. He ordered every chair except his own throne to be removed from the hall of reception so that Sir Thomas would be forced to stand in his presence throughout the interview. But our Ambassador was quick-witted. He whispered to one of his staff, who went down on hands and knees – and Sir Thomas sat on the seat provided. He also stood up to Cromwell. In 1653 he was recalled and a replacement was sent out, but Sir Thomas refused to leave. He stayed on until he was recalled by his King after the Restoration. Then he came back to Bower Hall, Steeple Bumpstead where he died in 1672.

The story of the Civil War has been detailed fully in the national histories. In Essex, the united front of the Eastern Association and its geographical position well away from royalist enclaves preserved it from battle and bloodshed. By the spring of 1648 Essex, leaders and labourers, was tired of the conflict, its ever-escalating cost and the damage it was doing to trade. At the Chelmsford assizes that spring a petition was raised and sent to Parliament, asking it to treat with the King for peace and to disband its army. Parliament rejected it, and when 2,000 men marched to Westminster to add vocal support to the petition, claiming that they represented the 30,000 inhabitants of the county, the Parliamentary leaders gave the Earl of Warwick a stiff warning of the consequences of further protest.

The army was as tired of the stalemate and the discomfort of daily living as were the civilians, but a new development was to alarm them. A union of Kent and Essex Royalists was effected at Shenfield on 8th June, with Sir Charles Lucas heading the Essex contingent. By the following day the Royalists had passed through Chelmsford to rendezvous with their Hertfordshire brethren at New Hall, Boreham. Next day, hearing that the Roundheads were following, they pushed on to Braintree, via the Earl of Warwick's own home – Leez Priory at Little Leighs. Despite the fact that he was their arch enemy, and he was not there to protect his wife, she reported, '. . . there was not anything touched; and they stayed only a dinnering time with me, and so marched on to Colchester.' They did take the arms they found about the place, but most weapons had been carefully hidden as soon as the servants heard of their approach. When they got to Braintree the Royalists heard that Fairfax and his army were at Billericay, so they decided to try to capture Colchester for the King. They reached the town during the afternoon of Monday 12th June – only just in time, for Fairfax was very soon within a mile of the town. There was a scuffle on the Lexden side before the Royalists could close and bar the gates. The Parliamentarians tried various ploys to effect an early entry, but after eight hours they had made no progress, and 1,000 of their men were killed.

The inhabitants, mostly Protestants and supporters of Parliament, endured a long siege. The Royalists knew they were virtually hostages who could be traded as a last resort, but in the end it was the Roundhead leader who deserted them, as we know from the diary of a Royalist which tells a moving story of the plight of the townsfolk as the siege dragged on into August:

> '1648 Aug. 2. The town was now in a miserable condition; the soldiers search'd and rifled the Houses of the Inhabitants for victuals; they had lived on Horse Flesh several weeks, & most of that also as lean as Carrion, wch. not being well salted bred wens; this want of Diet made the Soldiers sickley & many Died of Fluxes yet they boldly rejected all offers of surrender unless with safety of their Officers . . .
>
> Aug. 7. The Townspeople became very uneasy to the Soldiers, & the Mayor of the Town with the Aldermen, waited upon the General desiring leave to send to the Ld. Fairfax, for leave to all the Inhabitants to come out of the town that they might not perish . . . Ld. Fairfax refused ym.
>
> 12. The Rabble got together in a vast Crowd about the Ld. Goring's Quarters clamouring for a surrender; and they did this every evening; bringing women and children, who lay howling and crying on the Ground for Bread; the souldiers beat off the men, but the Women & Children would not stir bidding the Soldiers to kill them, saying they would rather be shot than be starved.'

A week later, after the few remaining horses had been given the thatch of houses to eat and the last dog had been stewed for the women and children, the Mayor, with the agreement of the Royalists' commander, begged the besiegers to allow the townsfolk, their supporters, to pass out of the town as refugees. Fairfax said they could do so if the prisoners-of-war came with them. The Royalists refused to give up their last card in this terrible war of attrition. So it was that the Royalists had to surrender unconditionally on 27th August.

The end was swift; the townspeople were already mixing with the

him to lead. At the Restoration it continued as the Coldstream Guards. Left as Commander-in-Chief in Scotland by Cromwell, he completed its subjection in 1652. Then appointed one of three 'Generals' of the Fleet, he outwitted the great Dutch admiral Tromp in actions in 1652 and 1653 and came back to the formal thanks of the House of Commons on 1st October 1653. Cromwell called him, 'Your honest General George Monck, who is a simple-hearted man.'

In 1659, just before the Restoration, the Royalists approached him for help in effecting the return of the monarch to the throne. He entered London at the head of his men on 3rd February 1660 and was solemnly thanked by Speaker Lenthall on behalf of Parliament. The Restoration was voted on 1st May 1660, after Monck disclosed his negotiations with Charles, whom he met on the shore at Dover on 25th May. Next day the King knighted him at Canterbury, and on 7th July gave him other titles, including Duke of Albemarle. He was granted a pension of £700 a year and the estate of New Hall, Boreham. When the rest of the army was disbanded his own regiment was retained as the King's personal guard. He devised the government which followed, 'Moderate, not rigid, presbyterian government, with a sufficient liberty for consciences truly tender.'

One Essex man suffered a very unusual and frightening penalty for his treason as a Parliamentarian once the King was again on the throne. He was Sir Henry Mildmay of the wide-spreading Essex family, of which an ancestor had described himself in his will, dated 1547, as a yeoman and merchant, and referred to the stall behind which he made his money in Chelmsford market. Sir Henry, knighted in 1617, bought the fabulous Wanstead House from George Villiers, Duke of Buckingham two years later. He was MP for Maldon for most of the years from 1625 to 1660 and espoused the Parliamentarian cause from 1641. As Master of the Jewel Office he was involved in some deceit concerning the crown jewels. At the Restoration he tried to escape abroad but was captured at Dover, tried and sentenced to life imprisonment with the added humiliation that, as one of Charles I's judges he should, every year on 27th January (the date of Charles' death sentence), be tied to a hurdle, with a hangman's noose around his neck, dragged by a horse to the place of execution, then dragged back again to prison in the Tower. It did not last for long as an annual spectacle; Mildmay produced a doctor's certificate declaring that he was ruptured and should not be subjected to such inhumane treatment. So he was banished to Tangier, though he actually died in Antwerp, in 1664.

THE RESTORATION PERIOD 1660–1714

10

Essex, through its prosperity and its proximity to London and to Parliament, had been an important key to the success of Parliament over kingly dictatorship and subsequently over an unruly army. It was now more united and independent as a county. Increasingly it became a place of residence for people important in national government and in commerce. At the same time the fertile soils, well watered by more than 22 rivers, became the market garden of London as it grew out into the Essex countryside. From now on the Essex farmer was in the forefront of agricultural innovation. Drovers herded their beasts from as far away as Wales to fatten on the Essex marshes before their arrival at the London markets.

Harwich was a key port at this time. Christopher Jones, who later became the famous master of the 'Mayflower', served on a jury in this town in 1605 when his stepfather appeared before the court for not keeping Lambard Stairs in good repair. The town's defences in general seemed to be in a similar state of disrepair in 1625 when it was reported by Sir Edward Coke that, '. . . all the ordnance is dismounted and the platforms decayed and the forts abandonned, so as a few Dunkirkers may without interruption enter that harbour . . . and then, landing a few men, may burn that rich town.'

In the same year the Duke of Buckingham went to Harwich for a ship to Holland. He was shown the defences and improvements were very quickly put in hand, with the rebuilding of Landguard fort a priority. Leonard Weaver, in *The Harwich Story* says, 'In Harwich and on the sea there was little of importance during the Civil War.' One reason may have been the edict issued by the Captains of six pro-Parliament Navy frigates in a meeting on board the *Providence* '. . . We write to the Mayor and defend against the common enemy, viz. the King's party, that then we will stand and act with them with all diligence, but if they comply or give way to the enemy to enter and possess the town we will use our uttermost endeavours to beat the enemies forth of the town again, though in doing so we beat down or fire the town.' No wonder that the Mayor and Aldermen reassured the parliamentarians of their loyalty to the cause.

Harwich continued through the 17th century as the principal port, dockyard and shipyard where the *Rupert* was built, launched in February 1666, of which Pepys, Secretary of the Navy, and a constant visitor to Harwich wrote, '. . . the King, Duke and everybody saying it is the best ship that was ever built.' After peace with the Dutch was concluded in December 1667 the Navy's base was closed, though ship-building continued. Samuel Pepys was made a Freeman of the Borough of Harwich and became MP for the town in 1679.

The City of London already dominated the distribution of cloth manufactured in weaving towns of Essex, and many of those clothiers were ruined when the London merchants went bankrupt in 1637. Trading into the heart of the capital brought news and ideas back out into the county, including the weekly newsletters being distributed in manuscript among circles of friends. One man regularly read just such a 'newspaper' out loud to an interested crowd in Colchester market.

At the Restoration in 1660 many of the clergy were reinstated in their former livings, and all members of government, from Parliament to borough officials and officers of the military, had to be proven communicants in the Anglican church. At this point the more puritanical members of that church, feeling they could no longer agree with its outlook, became 'Nonconformists'. Subsequently there were schisms which bred Congregationalists and Baptists. At Burnham-on-Crouch the Baptist records exist from 1673.

The Civil Wars had affected the lives of many an Essex man. One of them was William Harvey, of the well-known Hempstead family who, as Royal Physician to James I and Charles I, wrote his remarkable treatise *Exercitatio Anatomica de Motu Cordis et Sanguinis* which set out his epoch-making discovery of the circulation of the blood through the heart. It was not published until 1628, twelve years after he had confirmed his findings. During the Commonwealth he moved discreetly between his brothers' homes. One of them, Sir Eliab Harvey, had recently put in hand the building of a family vault in the parish church at Hempstead, so, on William's death in June 1657, aged 79, the corpse was carried in a great procession to that vault. When the church tower fell in 1882 the College of Physicians was so concerned about the safety of the remains of one of their most famous members that they paid for the re-interment of his lead-wrapped corpse in a sarcophagus of marble above the vault in the Harvey Chapel, crowned by a marble bust sculpted by Edward Marshall, which is claimed to be very true to life.

Woodham Mortimer Hall, home of Peter Chamberlen, Physician Extraordinary to Charles I and II.

Essex was the scene of another contribution to the world of medicine. Woodham Mortimer is a village most motorists speed through on their way to Maldon from the west. Few people know that one of the world's most useful medical inventions was conceived here and kept secret for 100 years. That invention was the forceps used to assist in cases of difficult childbirth. The inventor was Peter Chamberlen, born in 1601, a 'man-midwife' and a Fellow of the College of Physicians. He followed his uncle as Physician Extraordinary to Charles I and II. He stayed out of the turmoil of the Civil War at Woodham Mortimer Hall, out in the country but still within a day's ride of his practice in London. Here he brought up a family of 18 children by two wives.

His great success as obstetrician to royalty and society was entirely due to the use of his forceps. He delivered babies safely where, before, lingering labour often led to the death of baby and mother. His secret was the passport to his continued patronage by the wealthy. No-one was allowed to remain in the room when he had to use his forceps, so they could not divine how he so often saved baby and mother in forlorn cases. For 100 years, generations of Chamberlen doctors achieved fame and fortune from the secret forceps until at last an impecunious doctor sold the secret to a Dutch surgeon, who put the forceps into what we might term mass production. In 1813, the owner of Woodham Mortimer Hall discovered a hiding place under a floorboard, and there, in a wooden box, lay Peter Chamberlen's original forceps!

The dreaded plague struck again through 1665 and the following year. It was spread from London by traders and travellers along the highways through Essex. Colchester was hit particularly hard, with almost 5,000 people, a third of the population, dying from the infection. We have an on-the-spot account of the effect of the plague on an Essex village. Doctor Kidder was Rector of Rayne during a career which led him on to the Bishopric of Bath and Wells. 'My neighbours durst not come near,' he writes, 'and the provisions which were procured for us were laid at a distance upon a green before my house. No tongue can express the dismal calamity which that part of Essex lay under at that time. As for myself, I was in perpetual danger . . . I conversed daily with those who came from infected houses, and it was unavoidable . . . The provisions sent into the neighbouring infected town [Braintree] were left at the village where I was and near my house. Thither the Earl of Warwick sent his fat bullocks which he did every week give to the poor of Braintree. The servants were not willing to carry them any further. This occasioned frequent coming from that most infected place to my village, and indeed to my very door. My parish clerk had it when he put on my surplice, and went from me to his house and died. Another neighbour had three children, and they all died in three nights immediately succeeding each other and he was forced to carry them all to the churchyard and bury them. We were alarmed perpetually with the news of the death of our neighbours and acquaintances, and awakened to expect our own turns . . .'

The confused state of religious belief at this time is indicated by another comment from Bishop Kidder:

'About the year 1664 I settled at Rain [i.e. Rayne] . . . I came to a people that were factious to the greatest degree; that endeavoured to defraud the minister of his dues, and that were very censorious and given to separation, and great inveighers against the innocent rites and ceremonies of the church. I do not say they were all such; but there was much, too much of this leaven, and it had infected a great part of this side of the country.'

Suffice to say that religious belief had separated into the established religion of the Anglican Church with a mass of nonconformist groups on the one hand and the continuing old Catholic belief on the other. One local man caught in this tangle was the fourth Lord Petre, arrested

The ruins of St Botolph's church at Colchester – wrecked by gunfire in the Civil War. Nearby is the new St Botolph's built in 1838.

and sent to the Tower of London after the 'Popish Plot' of the notorious Titus Oates. His close imprisonment made him so ill that he died in 1684. Yet when the Glorious Revolution of 1688 was looming James II appointed that man's brother and successor to the position of Lord Lieutenant of Essex. In William and Mary's reign the pendulum swung again, Catholics were out of favour and the Toleration Act acknowledged the right to worship of those separate sects on the other side of the established church.

The problem of greatest concern to King and Parliament was the raising of money to fund the administration of the country as a whole. In 1662 an official advised the taxing of every hearth in every house, ranging from the humble hovel with its single hearth to the grand mansion of the famed General Monck, New Hall, which topped the list with 117 hearths. Since everybody had to have at least one fire for the daily cooking and to keep warm, the government should have gained considerable revenue, if everybody paid up; but they did not, and so they were taken to court. Take just one case:

> Eustace Seymour, tax collector, and Richard King, the constable at Leigh, went to the Quarter Sessions at Chelmsford to show how, on August 18th, 1669, they called at the houses of those who had not paid their hearth tax. One of them was the widow Elizabeth Motley. She would not answer the door, but stood behind it, putting her shoulder against it to prevent them opening it. Eustace pitted his strength against hers, forced the door open and grabbed the spit, a long meat skewer, with which the poor widow had armed herself. She then grabbed a kitchen knife and warned him to come no further. By this time a crowd had gathered round the door, taking the widow's side and threatening the two men. They escaped from the mob but they never did get the hearth tax from Mrs Motley, and that is why she ended up in court.

There is no doubt that money was desperately needed at this time. A military monument to this troubled period is Tilbury Fort. Planned first in Henry VIII's time, it was completely remodelled and re-armed in 1672 in response to the humiliating experience in 1667 when the Dutch fleet penetrated the Thames estuary, landed at Canvey Island to steal provisions, and then sailed on to take potshots at East Tilbury church tower. The shipyard at Harwich was very busy building ships to challenge such affronts, but there is nothing left to show just how important the government naval yard there was, except for the remarkable two-wheel treadmill crane built in 1667, and even that has been moved from its original position.

These were difficult times, too, for Parliament's management of the country. Charles II died in February 1685 and was succeeded by James II. Neither the Marquis of Argyll's invasion of Scotland, nor the Duke of Monmouth's landing at Lyme Regis, held much interest for the people of Essex. Nor did the landing of William and, later, the arrival of Mary, when they took over jointly from the discredited James II, from November 1688. William was wiser than James; he gained control through Acts which regularised meetings at Parliament, supported free worship for nonconformists and reduced the army in times of peace. He even deferred to Parliament in the matter of his own expenditure. Mary died in December 1694 from smallpox, aged only 33. William continued until 1702, finding it increasingly difficult to walk the line between the factions then emerging as the Tories and the Whigs. He died on 8th March 1702, Queen Anne ruled until 1714, then the House of Hanover made its mark in British and in Essex history.

ESSEX IN THE EIGHTEENTH CENTURY

The southern part of Essex suffered a disaster in 1707. There was a very high tide on 17th December. It overflowed the dyke which protected the little village of Dagenham from the tidal rising of the Thames. Thomas Moat, a Rainham carpenter, had the job of opening and closing the sluice gates which controlled the flow of water off the marshes behind the dyke. He opened one to get rid of the overflow and the hatch was smashed by the force of the water making a six-yard wide breach in the dyke which carried thousands of tons of earth out into the Thames. To mend it then would have cost some £30, but the delay caused by the bureaucracy involved in setting the work in hand allowed the tides to sweep in and out, causing a vast lake in the hinterland and taking more and more land out into the Thames, where it caused such sandbanks that they became a real danger to shipping. The 'Dagenham Breach' became famous. For 14 years it defied all attempts to repair. A special tax was voted by Parliament on all ships coming up the Thames to raise the sum required for the repair. Several contractors were beaten by the sheer force of the tidal flow through the breach, which widened to 100 yards and was 20 feet deep.

The government gave up, the breach became a vast lake, Essex landowners were in despair, Dagenham villagers saw the creek creeping up to their doorsteps. Then, like the hero in a melodrama, along came Captain Perry, a man skilled in such engineering work. It took five years, hundreds of workmen and an expenditure of over £40,000 to finally effect the repair in 1720. His book, *Account of the Stopping of Dagenham Breach* was published in 1721. There is still a lake left behind the embankment of the Thames, on the land now developed into a vast manufacturing complex by the Ford Motor Company.

By the time the Breach had been sealed, George I had been on the throne for 14 years. Under his influence Essex enjoyed a 'Golden Age' of farming. For many years farmers here knew about proper drainage, using marl or chalk to lighten the land, the growing of turnips and the rotation of crops which had put them well ahead of many other counties. Improvements in road-making and the construction of canals made travel and transport much easier and the population became increasingly mobile. An Act for the construction of the Stour Navigation was passed in 1705. During the century the Stort, the Lea and the Chelmer and Blackwater rivers were canalised.

New roads were paid for by the setting up of tollgates, or 'turnpikes'. Essex was adjacent to the City of London; business and pleasure in the capital was the merest coach or horseback journey away. It was not long before rich commuters were building elegant mansions such as Wanstead House practically within the sound of Bow bells. Sir Josiah Child, having made a fortune in the East India trade, bought the Wanstead House estate covering around 10,000 acres. His son, Richard, raised to the peerage as 1st Earl Tylney, put in hand the building of the grandest mansion, designed by Colen Campbell in the Palladian style, from 1715. The awful postscript to this particular manifestation of wealth and grandeur is that the family's financial imprudence meant that the place was mortgaged up to the hilt by 1800. It was decided that it was too near the ever-expanding metropolis and was put up for sale in 1822. It sold for just £10,000 to a speculator who demolished it, hoping to make a profit on the building material produced. The contents of the house realised over four times that amount.

The kind of life and entertainment which went on in these big houses is well illustrated by a handbill, printed and circulated through London and Essex, which announced:

AN

ACCOUNT

OF THE

STOPPING

OF

Daggenham Breach:

With the ACCIDENTS that have attended the same from the first UNDERTAKING.

CONTAINING ALSO

Proper RULES for performing any the like WORK: And PROPOSALS for rendering the Ports of DOVER and DUBLIN (which the Author has been employ'd to Survey) Commodious for Entertaining large SHIPS.

To which is PREFIX'D,

A Plan of the LEVELS which were over-flow'd by the BREACH.

By Capt. JOHN PERRY.

LONDON:

Printed for BENJ. TOOKE at the Middle Temple Gate in *Fleetstreet*, and Sold by J. PEELE, at *Lock's-Head* in *Pater-Noster-Row*. MDCCXXI.

Captain Perry's book, published in 1721, *Account of the Stopping of Dagenham Breach.* Perry succeeded where others failed in the long struggle to close the breach which eventually measured 100 yards wide and 20 ft deep.

'This is to give notice to all my honoured masters and ladies and the rest of my loving friends that my Lady Butterfield gives a challenge to ride a horse, to leap a horse, or run on foot or halloo with [i.e. chase] any woman in England seven years younger but not a day older because I won't undervalue myself being now 74 years of age. My feast will be the last Wednesday of April where there will be good entertainment for that day and all the year after in Wanstead in Essex.'

While the rich disported themselves away from prying eyes, the poor had to run the gauntlet of close-watching village gossips. If they made love outside marriage they had to pay for it. Today the words fornication and adultery have little meaning and less force, but a note in the parish register of Rettendon shows what a sin it was considered in 1717, and what a stir was caused in the little community.

'June 30th, 1717, Mary Rawbones and Ursula Everitt, singlewomen, and Mary Perry, widow, did penance in the parish church. The two former for committing fornication, the first with Ezekiel Carter, the second with Edward Lungley, both bachelors; and the third for committing adultery with John Robinson, a married man. A great multitude of people from all the neighbouring parishes being spectators.'

These guilty people had to dress from head to foot in white and carry white staffs. They stood facing the congregation throughout the service and then confessed their guilt and asked for forgiveness but only the women were judged guilty while the men went scot free.

Between rich and poor, a middle rank of farmers and merchants made a very good living from the London market. There was a constant and reliable demand for meat and dairy produce, for flour, oatmeal and barley. Market gardens were developed as near the capital as possible to reduce transport costs and to maximise freshness of the vegetables on the market stalls. It is hard to imagine the West Ham of today as a wide-spreading market garden, yet even before 1740 potatoes were being grown there on an experimental commercial basis, and the gardens spread out north and east, even as far as Rainham.

Fish to feed that hungry capital, particularly on days of religious fast, were caught by the great fleet of fishing boats based on Barking. It is such a commercial and industrial centre today, with buildings crowding down to the banks of Barking Creek where the river Roding joins the Thames that it is hard to believe that Barking was once a port of great significance. From its quay there sailed the greatest fishing fleet the world has ever seen. In 1814, when the quay had been rebuilt, 70 ships were tying up there, each of 40–53 tons.

The principal owner was Samuel Hewett. He gained fame and fortune for his family fishing firm, the Short Blue fleet, by introducing the first primitive refrigeration of the catch. It was organised like this: the marshes on the edge of the little town were flooded in the winter to provide ice. It was broken up and carted off to the Barking icehouse, a cavern dug deep in the earth where the ice was kept in usable condition right through the summer. On every fishing trip one ship loaded with ice went round the fleet collecting all the fish they had so far caught, and while that fleet carried on fishing the ice-ship hastened back up the Thames to London with a lucrative cargo of fresh fish. The high point in the history of the Short Blue fleet was in 1850 when all 225 fishing smacks sailed down the Thames and out to their fishing grounds. It was the introduction of rail transport which doomed Barking's role as a fishing port.

Further down the Thames, the chalk quarries at Grays have totally altered the riparian landscape. Millions of tons of earth have been carried away to be converted into lime and, latterly, cement. In 1669 Mr Samuel Irons was doing such good business in burning chalk for lime that he issued his own small change in the form of a halfpenny token on which he had impressed a drawing of a lime-kiln. The parish register records the burial of a 'lime-burner' in 1681. So we know that chalk has been quarried here for over 300 years. It would be quite impossible to estimate the amount removed. Two hundred years ago heavy loads of chalk were being carted in huge waggons with specially wide wheels along the miry Essex road to kilns up to 30 miles away.

Arthur Young, the eminent writer on agriculture, wrote in his *Tour Through the Southern Counties* published in 1757,

> 'Of all the accursed roads that ever disgraced this kingdom in the very ages of barbarism, none ever equalled that from Billericay to the 'King's Head' at Tilbury. It is for twelve miles so narrow that a mouse cannot pass by any wagon . . . the ruts are of an incredible depth except at a few places, and to add to all the infamous circumstances which occur to plague a traveller, I must not forget eternally meeting with chalk wagons, themselves frequently stuck fast until a collection of them are in the same situation, so that twenty or thirty horses may be tacked to each to draw them out, one by one.'

Daniel Defoe (1661–1731) author of *Robinson Crusoe*, set up a tile works at Chadwell. It prospered until he became too involved with his political writing, then it was closed down with a loss of £3,000, a very large sum at that time. He was having the same difficulties in finding workers as some employers complain of today, saying, 'I affirm of my own knowledge, when I have wanted a man for labouring work, and offered nine shillings a week to strolling fellows at the door, they have frequently told me to my face that they could get more a-begging . . .' He did not need to worry because his books were such a runaway success, though his political pamphlets did get him into trouble from time to time. Knowing Essex well, he set the opening scenes of *Moll Flanders* in Colchester, and later in life he leased the estate we know as Severalls so that his daughter Hannah could live there in comfort until her death in 1759.

Brick and tile making, introduced into the county by the Romans, was an art lost for hundreds of years. Its gradual reappearance is shown by a record of 1301 which shows a tiler was working in Colchester. In 1425 the General Council of Colchester published an edict that tiles should be made to standard sizes. Bricks have been produced in their millions in Essex since Tudor Times, to be exported well beyond the county boundary. Ingatestone Hall's brick exterior was completed by 1548. Pevsner says:

> 'The High Street has no house of independent value, but in the aggregate its Georgian brick and its fewer sixteenth and seventeenth century timber-framed houses form a happy picture.'

Wivenhoe Park, now part of the University of Essex, is a hybrid of such architecture, but in reverse. It was built between 1758 and 1761 in typical Georgian style, but almost a hundred years later it was altered and enlarged in a neo-Tudor style by the architect Thomas Hopper. The number of grand houses built in Essex by old-established families and up-and-coming London commuters is so great that they cannot be detailed in a general history. They have been surveyed by Nancy Briggs in *Georgian Essex* (1989).

While the tile and brick industry was growing, the great Essex cloth industry was declining. In 1700 the area of Braintree and Bocking was the second most important cloth-making centre in Essex, and a certain kind of cloth became known around the world as 'Bockings'. It had the reputation for hard-wearing quality which denim has today. Nearly 600 weavers took part in a strike in 1758, and many others would have carried on working. The unrest was caused by the huge loss of business to the new mills in the north of England with its threat to continuing employment in Essex. Men joined the Militia for alternative employment, and parents made sure that their children were not apprenticed to this dying trade.

Even as late as 1777 the weavers were marching through Braintree and

Bocking in their famous procession. Hundreds of them formed up on 1st April and marched together in commemoration of the establishment of the weaving industry in England in general and in Essex in particular. They carried aloft the flags of their country and their craft guilds, stepping in time to the brave music of a band. In front they carried, reverently, working models of the spinning and weaving inventions, like the wheel and the loom, representing the various branches of their industry. The newspaper tells us:

> 'They behaved with great decency throughout the whole, not one could be discerned to have been the least disguised in liquor; and most of the masters rewarded them with peculiar generosity, after which they discharged their bills, and retired quietly to work.'

An unusual but important Essex industry closely connected with cloth, was the making of a black dye and ink from copperas. The Portugese demanded black cloth for their women's wear, so Essex cloth workers with valuable export contracts with Portugal had urgent need of that dye. Copperas occurs naturally on the northeast coast of Essex as twig-like nodules of bisulphate of iron. It was gathered from the beaches by women and children, picking it laboriously from the foot of the cliffs where it had been washed out by tidal action. By mixing loads of copperas with layers of scrap iron and damping it all down, the deadly green vitriol, basis of the black dye, and sulphuric acid were produced. It was done on the foreshore, in hazardous conditions. At Walton-on-the-Naze the ground on which this was done became so polluted with sulphur that nothing grew there for over 100 years after the practice was discontinued. A traveller through Harwich in 1724 spoke of 'The famous well which turns wood into metal', continuing, 'I took out several pieces of sticks, which seemed to the eye to be wood, but were ponderous yet brittle. It is of this they make the best Copperas.'

Roads were improving all through the century. Sir Henry Bate-Dudley (1745–1824), editor of the *Morning Post*, squire of the village of Bradwell-juxta-Mare, and parson of that parish, used his influence as a Justice of the Peace to set in hand a county-wide improvement of the road system. He expended a great deal of his own money on making up the roads all around the village and also set a very good example of farm management. Though the traveller could make better time on the new roads, especially as new kinds of light, sprung carriages were being developed, they could not be said to be much safer. Highwaymen – a romantic name for petty thieves – like Essex-born Dick Turpin, preyed on travellers from hiding places in the forest borders of the road.

Legend has it that Turpin robbed the rich to give to the poor, but

Sir Henry Bate Dudley (1745–1824), squire and parson of the village of Bradwell-juxta-Mare, editor of *The Morning Post* and initiator of a county-wide improvement of the road system.

the fact is that most of his ill-gotten gains were spent on high living in low dives. He was born in Hempstead in 1705, where his parents kept the Bell Inn. Now it is known to the locals as Turpin's Tavern. He was apprenticed to a butcher in Whitechapel but was dismissed for bad behaviour. He joined a gang of rustlers, was identified and became a 'Wanted Man'. From then on he could only live by crime. He joined the Gregory Gang, desperadoes operating on the border of Essex with London.

The gang called on an old lady in Loughton and demanded her money. She told them to do their worst, and they picked her up bodily and held her over her own fire. In the agony of her scorching flesh she screeched out the hiding place of her life savings. The thugs dropped her on the floor, grabbed a haul of 400 sovereigns and disappeared into the night. They were villains, but they were horsemen too. Between dusk and dawn on a winter's night they rode from Chingford to Barking, a distance of 40 miles, robbing the vestries of both parish churches of everything valuable they could carry away.

By now Turpin had a price of £100 on his head for capture, dead or alive and other criminals would not risk working with him. He moved to a cave in Epping Forest from which he sallied forth to hold up traffic on the London to Cambridge road. His fame as a hero was short-lived. He shot dead a man, was recognised and fled. He hid out in Yorkshire, went to prison for poaching a pheasant and revealed his true identity by writing a letter to his brother which was intercepted by the authorities. He was executed on 7th April 1739.

'Essex saw less of the Hanoverians than their predecessors who had been attracted to their residences in the county and the delights of the royal forests,' says the historian Kenneth Neale. Nancy Briggs, in *Georgian*

Essex puts it another way, 'The early Hanoverians did not take more than a passing interest in Essex, for them Harwich was the gateway to the continent and their beloved Hanover.' An example of this was in September 1761 when Princess Charlotte of Mecklenburg – Strelitz disembarked at Harwich, spent the night at the house of the Marquis of Abercorn at Witham and two days later went on to her marriage to George III. It is surprising that the king was not more drawn to our very agricultural county, for he wrote pamphlets on agricultural improvement under the pen name of 'Ralph Robinson'.

The Peace of Paris of 1763 gave Britain colonial gains and the First British Empire was at its height of power, but, as far as Essex historians are concerned, an even more momentous event took place. It was the publication at Chelmsford of the county newspaper, which is still published today. Thanks to this continuity, it is a source of history which is denied to most other counties.

The Chelmsford Chronicle; or, Essex Weekly Advertiser first appeared on 10th August 1764, printed by William Strupar at premises 'opposite the Black Boy, in Chelmsford.' That very first issue declares, 'This number is to be as a specimen, and is given *gratis*.' It goes on: 'It has often been thought surprising that the county of Essex, which is one of the most considerable in England, should be without a newspaper, the source of information, and the channel of intelligence . . . The paper now offered to the public will remove this inconvenience . . . All manner of books, shopbills, catalogues, etc. will be neatly and expeditiously executed by the printer of this Chronicle, which will not be confined to articles of intelligence only, for variety of useful, instructive and entertaining matter shall be occasionally inserted in it, so that it will not be simply a news-paper but a repository of every kind of useful knowledge, and may not improperly be called THE FAMILY LIBRARY.'

The Peace of Paris the previous year had ended the Seven Years' War but the quarrel with the colonies was casting a shadow. The taxes which were levied to pay for that war were the cause of large-scale smuggling, with Essex men bringing in all sorts of goods from the continent. The customs men at Leigh-on-Sea had seized from smugglers' boats in that very year, thousands of yards of French lace, brocade, silk, cambric and lawn, together with quantities of silk stockings, pearls, jewellery and all kinds of rare goods from the burgeoning East India trade.

The value of the paper as a means of communication with the public at large was soon realised. Subsequent issues contained more and more advertisements. They range from the Chelmsford Races to be held on Galleywood Common to William Myers, staymaker, telling the ladies of the county that, though he had been unwell for the last two years, he had

The Chelmsford Chronicle first appeared on 10th August 1764, and soon became an indispensable source of news, cheaply available to those who could read.

now recovered and would be glad of their patronage.

News in October was more serious. The First Regiment of the Essex Militia 'went through their evolutions and firings with the greatest exactness.' A high tide at the end of September had not only damaged all the quays from London to the mouth of the Thames, but had also flooded the Barling marshes, drowned 100 of Mrs Bidler's sheep at Hullbridge and completely washed away Bridgemarsh Island, which had only recently been embanked.

The paper became an indispensable source of detailed county history, cheaply available to those who could read, telling the story of Essex as it happened. It maintained continuity through changes of ownership and name. It reported on meetings of the Essex Turnpike Trusts and of gentlemen and traders concerning the proposed canal from Chelmsford to Maldon. In 1768 it published a letter from a well known gentleman, Peter Muilman, suggesting that a county meeting be held, more than 100 years before the County Council was formed. In July 1770 we read, 'His majesty is graciously pleased to give the sum of one hundred guineas to be run for at Chelmsford in Essex, on the second day of the usual races by four years old mares, carrying eight stone and a half . . . And orders, as her majesty landed in Essex that this shall be called the Queen's Plate.'

Most books about Essex tell the story of Edward Bright, the Fat Man of Maldon – but few people have heard of his sister. It is thanks to the *Chelmsford Chronicle* of 16th August 1765 that we know that she was Mrs Sarah Suckling of Thaxted – 'a worthy widow Gentlewoman of an uncommon size'. When she died at the age of 47 she was reckoned to have weighed at least 20 stone – almost two and a half times the normal weight of a woman. The undertaker had to provide a double coffin and eight of the strongest men in Thaxted were asked to bear it to church. Even then there was doubt that they would be able to carry the coffin through the streets with dignity and respect, so they scoured the town for a low cart which could take a heavy weight and lowered the late Mrs Suckling on to it straight from her bedroom window, using her own pony to haul the cart up the hill to the church porch. The whole operation, we are told, 'was conducted with great decorum, considering the vast concourse of people.'

The complete record of our county was completed by the history written by the Reverend Philip Morant from earliest times to the start of the *Chronicle*. He died on 25th November 1770 and exactly 200 years later Mr R Powell, then editor of the *Victoria County History of Essex*, gave a public lecture on the man and his achievement. Morant was born in Jersey, educated in England, took up the curacy of Great Waltham in 1724, then moved on to Shellow Bowells, Broomfield, Chignal Smealey, St Mary-at-the-Walls in Colchester, Wickham Bishops and, finally, to Aldham in 1745.

The great work appeared in 1768, entitled *The History and Antiquities of the County of Essex*. Mr Powell got to the heart of our reason for gratitude to Morant – 'He finished the job!' – and that was what previous endeavours had failed to do; yet Morant was nearly 60 when he started. Though Philip Morant's remains lie in the old churchyard at Aldham, his tombstone has been brought into the chancel of the present church, where a window and a tablet remind the visitor of the contribution this humble rector made to Essex history.

Morant's excellent work was matched by a superb mapping of the county between 1772 and 1774 by John Chapman and Peter Andre resulting in the map of 1777. There had been other maps, of course, but none on a scale like this, of two inches to a mile. It was the first map to include features like mile stones, turnpike gates and green lanes.

It is a catalogue of the wealthy men of the county in that their houses are shown and their names engraved alongside. Many of them would have been present the following year, 1778, when, on 19th October, George III and Queen Charlotte arrived at Thorndon Hall as guests of the 9th Lord and Lady Petre, whence they proceeded the following day to review the troops assembled at Warley Camp. This was the first time that a Roman Catholic peer had been allowed to entertain the monarch of the realm. That summer another celebrity had been in camp with the militia at Warley. Dr Samuel Johnson stayed under canvas with his friend Captain Langton of the Lincolnshire Militia and watched the troops go through their drills and manoeuvres. He even went on the round of guards at midnight. As he was 69 years old at the time, it can be appreciated that he was active for his age. Noting the difference between the tents for officers and other ranks he said, 'The superiority of accommodation of the better conditions of life, to that of the inferior ones, was never better exhibited to me in so distinct a view.'

Dr Johnson makes the distinction between the classes; there are other illustrations of the gap between the rich and poor at this time. In 1772 Richard Choate, a grocer of Barnston, appealed to the Justices for help. Food prices had risen so steeply that even in this little village a group of starving inhabitants assembled, went into Choate's shop and threatened to attack him and his shop if he did not sign a written consent to sell them butter at sixpence a pound and cheese at threepence a pound. He did it, even though this was greatly under market price. Worse was to follow: Benjamin Foakes, landlord of an inn at Great Dunmow, came into the shop and demanded a whole cheese at that same price of threepence a pound. Choate said he would be bankrupted if he sold it at that price. Foakes' reply was that if he did not get the cheese he would get a mob from Dunmow to take a good deal more than the cheese. He left the shop, but then sent Thomas Gipson in with half a guinea, enough, he said, to buy 42 lbs of cheese. He bribed other people to do the same thing. Richard Choate saw his livelihood threatened and so sought the protection of the court.

In April of that same year waggons loaded with corn, meal and flour were stopped at Colchester by poor people 'in want of the common necessities of life'. They weighed the load into small quantities and sold it amongst themselves, at prices they could afford. The traders could not say their goods were stolen, but they did not get anything like the market price. The great crowd which had gathered let it be known that they would give the butchers' carts the same treatment when they came through. The demonstration spread down the road to Witham and on to Chelmsford, where another crowd seized two waggons of flour

The East India Company's military depôt at Warley. Originally intended, in 1805, as barracks for 2,000 cavalry, the buildings had long been unoccupied when they were purchased by the company in 1842.

and took them to the market-place where they sold it to allcomers at 1s. 6d. a peck. The millers, including the well known Marriage family, the butchers and the bakers accepted the reduced prices, not only to express their sympathy for the poor but also to avoid the possibility of a serious riot.

Meanwhile the war with the American colonies was not going well and Essex suffered in the taking by the press gangs of many of their fishermen and merchant sailors for service in the Royal Navy. September 1783 brought the Peace of Versailles and the loss of those American colonies. Full details in the *Chronicle* pushed local news off the page, while advertisements continued as numerous as ever, some of them inserted by the government, like the announcement of prizes in the state lottery, and the sale by auction of a vast amount of spirits seized from smugglers and lodged in the Harwich custom house.

In January 1784 the weather was so bad that the newspaper declared:

'Let the rich, who cannot as present live without large fires in every part of their house, without flannels, wrappers and great coats, reflect on the deplorable state of many thousands who are well nigh deprived of the use of their limbs for want of these comforts.'

The industrial revolution was already turning its crushing wheels; Essex clothworkers were suffering from the mechanisation in the northern mills while Sir Richard Arkwright, with his own property in Essex, '. . . is supposed to have increased his property at least £20,000 per annum by his invention of the machines called Spinning Jennies.' 1791 brought the news that Essex farmers had sown Egyptian wheat on land around London in a successful experiment. The big event in the county town was the news that on 13th January 1792 'The Shire House Committee made their final report that that public structure had been completed in the most perfect and elegant manner, with a saving of near 2,000 pounds under the original estimate . . .' John Johnson, the county surveyor and architect of the Shire Hall, was publicly thanked and given 'a piece of plate' worth 100 guineas.

Chelmsford's role as the county town had been established before the 13th century, through the fact that the Manor was vested in the Bishop of London. Its position in the centre of the county also recommended Chelmsford as the most convenient place for the holding of the courts of the Royal Itinerant Justices. Records show that these courts were held spasmodically from 1189 and regularly from 1226. In 1199 the Bishop, as Lord of the Manor, obtained a royal licence to hold a weekly market and an annual fair.

By the 14th century the town was of settled importance and reputation. In old documents one can see mention of a wide range of trades and professions, showing the place catered for the demands of a wide area around it. A new bridge over the Can, at the bottom of the High Street, was built in 1382 to the plans of Henry d'Eveley, the architect who designed the nave of Westminster Abbey. What a stir must have been caused when Henry VII and his retinue stayed in Chelmsford in the course of a Royal Progress in 1489. He summoned the gentlemen of Essex to meet him there, telling them to be '. . . well-appointed, so that the Lancashire men might see that there were gentlemen of so great substance in Essex that they could buy all Lancashire'.

It was thanks to a later Lord of the Manor, Thomas Mildmay, that we have the excellent map of the town made by John Walker in 1591. It gave the Mildmays an idea of the extent and state of their property, but we value it also for the written summary by this meticulous surveyor which gives such a vivid description of the town at this time. It concludes: 'Not far distant from [the] parish church is one other fair building called the market cross or Session House, very convenient and necessary before the Justices themselves, their under officers and ministers, and also for all sorts of subjects to be attendant there, as well as for the common Gaol and prisoners, so as all may commodiously serve to their convenient ease in the same.' That Session House survived until 1791. In 1787 the bridge had to be renewed. The date carved on its keystone can still be read today. Both these rebuildings were designed and supervised by John Johnson, the surveyor to the county.

The threat of invasion at the end of the century, during the Napoleonic wars resulted in barracks being built in the town beside the gaol, down by the river and in Wood Street on the site of St John's Hospital. Entrenchments, big gun emplacements and other fortifications were thrown up, overlooking the roads an invading force would traverse. This is why there is no Moulsham Hall today and the story is as follows:

When the ruling family at Chelmsford, the Mildmays, married into the Fitzwalters, the premier barony of England, they aspired to a mansion worthy of their high place in society. So they tore down the beautiful Tudor house in which they had lived for 200 years and had a new mansion built on the site. In 1770, Lord Fitzwalter, as he was then, was often away from home on national business. When he did return to Chelmsford they rang the church bells to welcome him – that is how important he was! This grand house was inherited by a Miss Mildmay who married Sir Henry Paulet St John. He had to take her father's name and also to undertake to live in the house at least three months in every year. This was a great inconvenience since he already had his own house; then a curious coincidence occurred. The military authorities needed a house, just far enough away from the coast to serve as a headquarters in the event of a French invasion. Moulsham Hall fitted the bill exactly. They wanted to lease it, but that three months of compulsory residence by Sir Henry was the stumbling block. The problem was easily solved; the government had a special Act of Parliament passed to cancel this obligation and the military were installed. When they finished with it in 1808 Sir Henry had the house razed to the ground and all the furniture and pictures were sold. Now a large housing estate straddles the site.

Colchester claims on its town signs that it is the oldest town in Britain. Its first charter, after its ancient, Roman importance, was granted in 1189. It flourished as the staple town, the principal place for control of quality and for sale of cloth over a wide area of northern Essex. The siege of Colchester in 1648 rang the death knell of that industry. While Chelmsford may claim the dignity of County Town, Colchester is its superior in size and population and in the magnificence of its museum collections, particularly of its great Roman past. It has also played an important part in military history as a garrison town since the Napoleonic Wars. In recent years it achieved further distinction as an enlarged borough which includes the University of Essex at Wivenhoe Park. A quotation from G H Martin's *Official Guide to Colchester* points up the inevitable price which must be paid by this busy Essex town to meet the 21st century: 'The town's shops were extensively rebuilt, often erasing ancient boundaries and obliterating, with concrete beams and plate glass, the irregularities that mark old buildings and streets. Above all, motor traffic increased, demanding more and more empty space to rest in, and a perfect forest of notices on poles to advise, direct, and admonish its drivers. The most important change was probably the introduction of a one-way traffic scheme in 1963, that swept the Saturday market out of High Street, and turned a place in which people had lingered and gossiped for more than a thousand years into a conduit for smoke and hot metal.'

The Borough of Maldon has one distinction in common with Colchester. They both had their charters as boroughs withdrawn for a period, because of electoral corruption. Colchester's period without the valuable charter lasted 21 years from 1742. Maldon was penalised in 1768 and did not get its borough status back until 1810. It has always been a busy little town on the estuary of the Blackwater, but its business

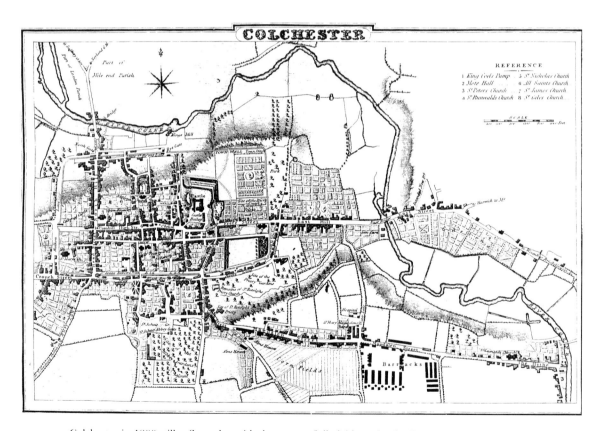

Colchester in 1800 still reflects the grid plan so carefully laid out by the Romans.

men and merchants made a fatal error in that period when they lacked the charter. They would not join in the building of the Chelmer and Blackwater Navigation, the canal, using the rivers from Chelmsford to the estuary where sea-going vessels could tie up. As a result the backers bypassed Maldon and took the canal on round to Heybridge. Over the period between its opening in 1797 and the advent of the railway system from 1845, the canal business flourished. Factories like Bentall's went to Heybridge and Maldon did not develop beyond the status of a local market centre with barge traffic to and from its hythe.

It could be said that Witham also lost its chance to develop through a source of water. In this case, though, it was a simple spring. A certain Dr Taverner had discovered that this spring, rising within three quarters of a mile of the town, was rich in mineral salts. He had seen how fortunes had been made from such streams at Bath and Tunbridge Wells, where everybody who was anybody went to 'take the waters' and at the same time lead a busy social life. So, in 1737, Taverner advertised his prospective Witham Spa with a pamphlet which told the world how this chalybeate spring produced water which quickened the blood and 'dissolved viscid humours'. He claimed it was a spa even before the pump room and associated buildings had been erected, and he was so convincing that businessmen in Witham smartened up their shops and inns to attract the patronage of all those who would be heading for the spa. That is why you can see, above today's shops the old buildings fronted in characteristic Georgian symmetry. Sad to say, the Witham spa did not gain enough custom to continue long in business. Dr Taverner died in 1748 and the spa died with him.

Harwich's history as the 'Gateway to the continent' has been touched upon, but little has been said of the way in which the old port nearly dug its own grave at the beginning of the 19th century. Around 1812 it was found that a kind of cement-stone could be quarried from the cliffs, broken up, burned in a kiln, then ground to a fine powder. Used as fresh as possible, it was mixed with sand and water to a paste called Roman cement. It would set even under water. For such a useful concretion demand soared. It was a vital ingredient in the construction of the great redoubt called Landguard Fort on the other side of the harbour. Those military engineers installed a mill to crush the cement-stone on such a grand scale that they processed over 200,000 tons before leasing it out for commercial exploitation.

Everybody wanted this miracle cement. For example, it was employed as a damp-proof stucco for the thousands of Regency houses then being built in London. So the manufacturers went on cutting away the cliffs at Harwich to get at the stone. Once this bulwark of harder material was removed the soft cliffs were easily eroded by the sea and a whole headland, where the stone breakwater stands today, disappeared under the ocean. At one time it seemed that the sea might break through behind the town and thus cut it off completely from the mainland. At last the Corporation acted: digging stone at the foot of the cliffs was forbidden and sea defences were put in hand. What really saved the town from the sea was the invention of Portland cement, which used chalk for its catalyst, and the best chalk was found at Grays. Portland cement was cheaper and stronger, so Harwich and its cement-stone were fortunate survivors.

The story of Braintree is set out in the wonderful murals in the former Town Hall, now the home of the Braintree Heritage Trust, painted by Maurice Greiffenhagen on huge copper plates set all round the Council Chamber. The building, to the design of Vincent Harris and at the expense of Sir William Courtauld, was opened in 1927.

In 1826 artist Robert Crane produced an illustration of 'all the prominent figures who frequented Braintree market' outside the Horn Inn. It was engraved as an aquatint by a man called Reeve at the expense of Thomas Nottidge of Bocking, High Sheriff. It was impossible for the artist to hold up traffic and business in the market while he painted each person – at least 31 recognizable individuals are shown – so he listed them and then called at their homes and at his leisure and theirs made water-colour studies of each one. He then made a large oil painting of the market place, setting all his subjects in suitable groupings. The engraver copied the painting on a reduced scale and the sepia impressions from the copper plate were coloured by hand. They included Doddy Hayes, the dwarf who sold shellfish, and Ben Patmore who brought his hot pies of meat or fruit to market in a wheelbarrow. The pies sold at a penny a time, but Ben was always ready to toss with his customers double or quits, though the number of lucky customers who got a pie for nothing were very few! The huge figure to the right of the picture is 'Great John Digby', with a mouth so wide and a voice so loud that when he cried his mackerel in the market he could be heard at Coggeshall, six miles away.

Southend-on-Sea is now the home of so many great commercial enterprises that it would be invidious to single out any particular name. Until local government reorganisation in 1974 it was the only county borough in Essex, and by far the largest town, with a population of around 170,000. To think that it all started in the south of the old parish of Prittlewell, with the building in 1767 of a few cottages called Pleasant Row. They became holiday homes for discerning folk who liked the sea air and the solitude where the Thames was embraced by the North Sea.

138

An engraving from an oil painting by Robert Crane, depicting the notable figures who frequented Braintree market in 1826 – there are up to 31 recognizable characters.

By 1794 Thomas Archer of Prittlewell, a priest, wrote a poem – 304 lines of rhyming couplets – in praise of the 'New South-end'. Though it was, by then, hardly developed at all, he prophesied:

> 'Streets shall extend and lofty domes arise,
> Till NEW SOUTH-END, in each spectator's eye
> With Weymouth, Margate or Brighthelmstone vie.'

He anticipated the roads which would take the ever-increasing traffic:

> 'Down the New Road they post with swift career
> In coach and four, or humble one-horse chair.'

Today we can heartily agree with a couple of his closing lines:

'Whether for health, for pleasure or for sport,
The various train to NEW SOUTH-END resort.'

Or, as the county newspaper put it in August, 1792, 'The new Sea-bathing village of South End, in Essex, at this time, overflows with aquatic visitants.'

On the national front, though, the news was serious: 'The black cloud of war, which hangs so heavily, this summer, over the Continent of Europe, more and more lowers ...' France, Russia, Prussia, Holland, Belgium, Poland and Britain were all engaged in battles on land and sea over the next 20 years or so. At the same time 500 children, celebrating the sixth anniversary of the establishment of Sunday Schools in Colchester, walked in procession to church. Through such schools many underprivileged children learnt to read and write.

In the wake of the French Revolution, meetings were held all over Essex to demonstrate loyalty to our King – even little Goldhanger turned out in a body to sing patriotic songs and burn an effigy of Tom Paine, author of *The Rights of Man*.

In 1800 the children of the day were chanting, 'Chelmsford church and Writtle steeple fell down one day but killed no people.' The fact is that the church at Chelmsford collapsed during the night of 17th January because workmen who had dug a grave under the pavement of the aisle had made the hole much too close to a pillar. In the night the pillar slipped into the hole and brought the roof crashing down. It took a special rate on the inhabitants and a lot of argument from nonconformists about such an imposition before repairs could be effected. It was in April that Writtle church tower collapsed; the jangling bells leaned outward for a brief moment, then all came down with a most tremendous clangour. A far worse tragedy was the huge explosion at the Powder Mills at Waltham Abbey on 1st February 1802 when they were in full production on a war footing. Nine people and four horses were killed, their pathetic remains scattered over a wide area.

Many an Essex sailor served under Nelson at the Battle of Trafalgar. The great man's death in victory was fully reported in the county newspaper of 11th November, 1805, only 21 days after the actual event. News of the Battle of Waterloo was published within five days; 'DEFEAT OF BONAPARTE – The melancholy part of this news is the price in blood which it has cost.'

Life went on, and there was no stopping human ingenuity. A gas lighting scheme for private subscribers had been introduced in Chelmsford as early as 1815. Within three years a plan for lighting the town by gas

The view from 'Southend Terrace' in the parish of Prittlewell in 1830 – the beginnings of the modern day resort.

had been put forward and 'spiritedly entered into by the inhabitants; and had not individuals been limited as to the number of shares they should take, the subscription would have been filled instantaneously.'

The newspapers went into mourning with heavy black borders to announce the death of George III at 8.35 pm on 29th January 1820. He had been mentally ill in 1788, due possibly to porphyria, but it was not until 1810 that this illness struck again, and incurably. The sad old King was nearly 82 when he died. His son had been Prince Regent from 1812 and succeeded him as King George IV.

The common people of Essex have always had a great sense of fairness. It was demonstrated clearly on the occasion of the death of Queen Caroline, whom George IV had married in 1795. This was no love match; the King only married her as a sop to Parliament so that it would pay off his enormous debts. Their baby Princess Charlotte was born in January 1796, and then they parted. Caroline went off to Italy and her paramour, but on her husband's coronation in 1820, came back, demanding her place as Queen. She tried to attend the coronation, but was turned away at the door of Westminster Abbey. Broken in health and spirit, she died on 7th August 1821.

The King was out of the country. His ministers knew he would not want a great fuss made about her death, yet the common people were very much on her side. Since Caroline's body was to be taken to her old German home for burial, the government arranged that she should be taken to Harwich in a hearse drawn by eight horses followed by 26 carriages for the representative mourners. The route was planned to circumvent the City of London and its mob which could so easily be aroused. Though Caroline had specifically directed that she did not wish to have a military escort, the government thought it was essential, and they were right. Hardly had the procession started when a great crowd blocked the road at Hyde Park and the escort had to find an alternative route.

Then the cortège headed for the Great Road, today's A12, to pass through Ilford, Chelmsford and Colchester. At Ilford crowds caused more trouble as they shouted insulting criticism of the King in his treatment of his poor queen. Night was falling as they approached Romford. It had been planned to stop there for the night, but the inhabitants turned out in force, lit their torches and insisted on escorting the corpse all the way to Chelmsford, where the coffin was rested reverently in the church. Next morning great crowds saw the funeral procession off on the road to Colchester, where the next night was spent. Even though the coffin was again placed in a church for protection, somebody gained access and fixed a placard on it declaring, 'Here lies Caroline of Brunswick, the injured Queen of England.' The organisers were glad to head for Harwich next morning and see Caroline's catafalque safely aboard the frigate *Glasgow*, and headed for Brunswick and burial.

In 1825 the first steam-driven train ran on the Stockton to Darlington railway and as early as 7th January of that year a 'New Rail Road' from London to Norwich was already being suggested, though the coach masters announced their implacable opposition. In 1827 John Constable was busy on such paintings as the *Haywain* and *Dedham Lock* which brought the beauty of Essex and Suffolk to an admiring world. Some of these paintings are preserved in the National Gallery.

The most important event of that year was the passing of the Reform Bill. Until that time members of the House of Commons came largely from the south and there was a good deal of corruption in electoral matters. In the reorganisation Essex gained two seats as a county and the qualifications for voters were set to include a much wider range of people, in a scheme which stayed in force down to 1867.

From the aftermath of the Napoleonic wars down to the 1830s there was much unrest amongst the agricultural labourers of Essex.

In 1816 Sible Hedingham was a village with shops serving a wide area of agricultural land worked by vast teams of labourers and horses, but ingenious men were inventing machines for doing work on the farm much more quickly and efficiently. This meant that farmers could dismiss much of their work force and multiply their profits, quickly recovering their capital investment in the machines. Those poor labourers, with large families, had relied on the farmer for their food and shelter. By using machinery the farmworkers felt he was breaking his trust with them, and reducing them to abject poverty. They met together in secret, went into the barns and the fields at night and broke the machines that were breaking them. One farmer heard them, called out the constable and he arrested the ringleaders. He was taking them off to prison when their fellow agitators cornered him in a shop in Halstead. They smashed the windows, rescued their workmates and then went on the rampage, smashing windows all through the town. Men in neighbouring villages soon heard of the uprising and hastened to Halstead in support. The Halstead Cavalry and the 20th Regiment of Dragoons at Colchester were called out, and special constables were quickly sworn in from the ranks of the shopkeepers and the richer inhabitants. All roads in and out of Halstead were sealed off, the revolt was quelled, the leaders went to prison and the younger generation looked to towns and their trades for a better life in the Victorian era.

Another riot, for an altogether different reason, broke out in East Ham churchyard, one dark night in 1830. Two body-snatchers, or Resurrection men as they were then called, had crept in to dig up the corpse of a seven-year-old girl for sale to the surgeons at a teaching hospital. This was then a lucrative trade. The dead girl's father had suspected that such an attempt would be made and had kept watch with two friends and his dog. The men tackled one of the thugs and the dog took a grip on the other one's leg. He screamed 'Help, murder!' hoping that people abed would be roused to come to his help, cause a diversion and thus allow him to escape. At this time there was a colony of Irish folk living in the neighbourhood of the church. They came tumbling out, and saw the true situation in a trice. While the men set about the two thieves the women took off their stockings, filled them with stones and, says the newspaper, 'struck the prisoners on the head, until their bodies were almost applicable to their own trade.' They were committed to the Barking House of Correction to await trial at Chelmsford Assizes.

In 1830 also, on 26th June, George IV died and was succeeded by William IV, the 'sailor king', whose brief reign ended with his death on 20th June 1837, just one month after the 18th birthday of his niece Victoria, his successor.

12

VICTORIAN AND EDWARDIAN ESSEX

The reign of Victoria was one of transition. The Queen's accession in 1837 marked the end of the Georgian age; at the end of her reign, the First World War was only 13 years away. Essex suffered many changes. Two powerful reasons for this were the growing urbanisation of all the area contiguous to London and the terrible agricultural depressions caused by foreign imports, together with the unemployment caused in the countryside by ever-increasing mechanisation on the farm.

The topography of the county was irredeemably altered by the grading, embanking and bridge-building necessary to the introduction of railways. A forecast of what was to come is seen in the sale catalogue of 7th May 1839, when the Mildmay family disposed of most of the Essex property acquired by their 16th century forefathers – merchants and politicians of such acumen that they rose to the ranks of the rich and noble, served the King and filled their pockets. The 36 page catalogue details 430 acres of freehold land in the 'Capital and improving Market and Assize Town of Chelmsford . . . having the immeasurable advantage of a rail road from London, called, The Eastern Counties, now in full progress, and promising every reasonable expectation of being opened next year for public conveyance as far as the town of Chelmsford.' Like all good sale catalogues it was more optimistic than accurate; the first trip along the line built out from London via Romford and Brentwood to Chelmsford was that made by directors and engineers in 1843, fully described in *The Rivers Chelmer and Blackwater*. The impact of this new form of transport on the townspeople is shown in an anonymous poem on Chelmsford in 1845, touching on the amazing addition to the landscape of the viaduct:

> 'And yonder where in close succession rise
> Arch after arch inviting our surprise,
> There runs the Railway – hark! that piercing cry!
> The engine with its ponderous train draws nigh;

An engraving from *The Illustrated Times* of 26th July 1856. The choice of the town as the venue for the Royal Agricultural Society's exhibition that year reflected the importance of the recently built railway link with the capital.

Onward it comes with twenty horses's power
With speed at rate of fifty miles per hour . . .'

The work of the railway 'navvies' went ahead at such a rate that the line had reached Colchester by May 1843, and continued on to Norwich, at a cost of some £57,000 a mile, which was a colossal sum at the time. Much of the expense arose from demands for compensation to landowners. Through this period a web of branch lines was woven through the countryside, including villages like Chappel. Once this village had the charming name of Pontisbright, from the bridge (Latin – *pons*) which Beorhtric built across the Colne in the 11th century. A chapel had been built here for the convenience of the growing number of worshippers who could not cross to Wakes Colne church when the river was in full flood. The architect of the other 'bridge' which crosses the river here,

145

Chappel Viaduct, built in 1847 by the Colchester, Stour Valley, Sudbury and Halstead Railway. Constructed from bricks made locally at Bures, the viaduct is the largest in East Anglia.

the magnificent railway viaduct, is not recorded locally at all. Yet this viaduct of 30 arches, the largest of them 75 ft high, has been estimated to have needed some seven million bricks to carry the railway that short but essential 320 yards. It was the largest viaduct ever built for the Great Eastern Railway and is the biggest in East Anglia. It has been called, 'the most imposing Victorian architectural monument in the county.'

As soon as Queen Victoria was crowned in June 1838 her advisers were exercised to arrange a suitable marriage. She married Prince Albert in February 1840 when they were both 20 and produced nine children as evidence of their wedded bliss. Yet there was a man in Essex who found fault with them. Charles Clark, tenant of Totham Hall was studying birth control at a time when it was quite a wicked thing to do. He spent long candlelit nights around 1840 printing leaflets on birth control, which included much poetry. Some of them he tied to gas-filled balloons and sent them on windblown journeys of propaganda.

146

He was a bachelor who fervently believed his county, and his country, was becoming overpopulated. The remedy, he stated, must be birth control. He even dared to comment on the regular royal births. He wrote and printed a revised version of the national anthem which runs:

> 'God stop quick Vic. our Queen!
> O! thwart our fruitful Queen –
> God stop the Queen!'

He produced good verses, too, like *An Essex Calf's Visit to the Tiptree Races* which gives a fascinating picture of mid-Victorian Essex rural life. He combined with his neighbour to write and print a history of Great Totham which is now a collector's item. He died in 1880; Queen Victoria grandly reigned on.

The developing depression in agriculture hit the country in general and Essex in particular. The plaque set in the wall of Tudor Cottage, Greensted Green, near Ongar, says 'On their return from transportation the Tolpuddle Martyrs, George Loveless, James Loveless and James Brine lived here from 1838 to 1844.' What did they do to merit this special mention? With three other agricultural labourers, they formed a trade union to resist the reduction of their wages by a farmer in Tolpuddle, Dorset, in 1834. After a travesty of a trial, the men were sentenced to transportation to Australia for seven years. The public outcry was so great that in less than two years a full pardon was granted, and they were brought back to Britain. A fund subscribed by the general public gave them a seven-year lease of New House Farm in Essex, but in the face of continuing hostility from local farmers the men and their families emigrated to Ontario.

There was a great spirit abroad during this age, working to ameliorate the conditions in which poorer people lived and died. One cause of death was the infection of the water supply. The rapidly increasing population of towns and villages in the neighbourhood of London not only

The benefits of using The *Chelmsford Chronicle* to carry advertisements quickly become recognised. Here are some examples from the newspaper in 1870, reflecting the development of agricultural machinery in Victorian times.

147

put a strain on the limited amount of water available from springs, wells and ponds but also led to diseases being spread rapidly. In the 1770s Southend was a growing seaside town quite independent of the old, mother village of Prittlewell. All the new estates on the clifftop and the hinterland were supplied with water brought up from deep in the chalk substratum and filtered to a high standard of purity. The Prittlewell people did not want to pay for the connections they would need to this new system. It would mean the digging up of roads and knocking about of their houses to lead the water in.

So the old, laborious task of taking buckets to the pump, or hauling up water from the well, continued right up until 1880. In that year there was such a heavy fall of rain that it flooded the streets and made the primitive cesspools overflow. The sewage seeped underground into the supplies for the village pump and people's private wells. The villagers were not aware of the calamity until at least twelve of them fell ill with typhoid. The authorities acted swiftly, the village pump was locked up and the use of private wells was strictly forbidden. The Southend Water Company was asked to deliver its water to the village in water carts. Prittlewell people were persuaded that if they had to have the company's water, they might as well have it through the miraculous pipes which delivered it right into the kitchen sink.

In 1868 the village of Terling lost 44 inhabitants to typhoid fever and at least 300 others were seriously infected. All wells were closed; a new, pure source of water was led from a spring in Swan Pond through 16 standpipes throughout the village. The water was pumped by a water wheel driven by the stream which had caused the infection. This was the village water supply down to 1916.

The established church was beginning to lose touch with the poorer people, while the power of preaching in Nonconformist chapels brought in converts. The most famous Essex preacher of the time must surely be Charles H Spurgeon (1834–92), born at Kelvedon, who was strongly influenced by his Calvinistic grandfather, minister of the Independent chapel at Stambourne from 1811 to his death in 1864. Spurgeon started his ministry in Waterbeach, Cambridgeshire, and then went on to preach at the Metropolitan Tabernacle in Newington Causeway to congregations of 6,000 at a time. For nearly 30 years this huge following stayed faithful to him. It is said that his sermons, circulated in print, totalled some 50 million copies.

Away to the southeast of the county there was a much more humble and modest flowering of Essex faith. The name of Chapel Cottages in North Street records the chapel of the Peculiar People, a sect now merged into the Union of Evangelical Churches. It started when James

Banyard, a humble shoemaker in Rochford, went to listen to a pair of evangelists who were preaching in the town. Their simple message of belief based on the Bible caught his imagination, and inspired him to preach amongst friends and acquaintances. His congregation grew rapidly and they built their own chapel in 1838. They called themselves 'Peculiar' in the sense that their set of beliefs was peculiar to their congregation, including healing through anointing with oil and the laying on of hands. The message spread over a small area either side of the Crouch and further chapels were built. Today they are unusual homes in which the owners may still sense the simple faith of those country people. They carried the dishes and bowls containing their Sunday dinners to the Chapel and put them on the chapel stove to warm up while they spent the day in prayers and praise.

The old churches of Essex were admired by Alfred, Lord Tennyson. He often walked the wooded ways of Epping Forest between 1837 and 1840, remembering in *In Memoriam* how:

'The Christmas bells from hill to hill
Answer each other in the night.'

and how:

'A single church below the hill
Is pealing, folded in the mist.'

That church was the abbey church of Waltham Holy Cross.

It is fascinating to see from the history of just one house how Essex has changed. Henry VIII granted the deer park at St Clere's Hall, Danbury to his brother-in-law William Parr, who sold it on to Sir Walter Mildmay. On this land Mildmay built the house call Danbury Place. Here his heir Sir Humphrey Mildmay, born 1593, lived in great style.

After Sir Humphrey's death the house passed through several hands and the estate was split up, until Danbury Place was reduced to the status of a mere farmhouse, and dilapidated at that. When John Round bought it, in 1831, he pulled it down and replaced it with the present house, known as Danbury Palace. He employed the famous architect Thomas Hopper, but his wife Susan also had a lot to do with the design, not only to make it as picturesque as possible, but also to ensure that three staircases were installed, one of them to be entirely of stone, for she had a great fear of being trapped in a fire. Yet she did die in a fire – in a London hotel. Her husband could not contemplate living in the house after her death. He put it up for sale in 1845 and it was bought by the church to serve as the Palace for the Bishop of Rochester, in whose diocese Essex was included. It was sold again in 1892 and the new owner cut down no less than 429 oak trees, changing the character of the place beyond recognition.

The Palace, with its own private chapel, continued to be lived in right down to the Second World War, when the owners put most of the rooms at the service of the government for a hospital. At the height of the Blitz many a London mother-to-be was brought here to have her baby in the safety of the old Bishop's Palace, which served as a maternity hospital throughout the war. It was finally bought by Essex County Council to serve as a management training and conference centre, so the park and the pleasant lakes and copses are now sure of preservation for public access.

From big houses to small. We see the growing concern of Victorian employers for their workers demonstrated by the Courtauld family. Samuel Courtauld founded a silk-weaving factory in Braintree, and

These Courtauld Company houses in Church Street, Bocking, were built in 1872. Samuel Courtauld, the founder, was part of a more widespread change in the attitudes of the Victorian employers towards their workers.

trebled its size in 1817 before moving on to Bocking, where the watermill provided all the power he needed. Here he introduced the manufacture of crape much used in Victorian funeral and mourning dress. So successful was he that he was able to buy and convert the Town Mill in Halstead to make crape on contract. He soon doubled his work force – good news indeed for the many people who had lost their jobs on the land through mechanisation and falling farm prices. Courtauld built houses for his workers, many of them still bearing the firm's monogram worked into their gables. Samuel Courtauld once said, 'When I die, I should like to have written on my tomb, "He built good cottages."' By the time he died in 1881, in his 88th year, he was held in the highest esteem by his employees. He and his wife, it was said, '. . . looked after the welfare of their workpeople, and were untiring in their efforts for the education, amusement, sustenance and good housing of every man, woman or child whom they employed.' Those work people responded in 1846 by arranging a special dinner in a huge marquee next to the family's home at High Garrett in Bocking Street. During the course of it they presented him with a silver medallion and an illuminated address. It was estimated that some 5,000 people filed past, four-abreast, workers and their families come to honour their employer. It is unlikely that such a sight will ever be seen again in Essex.

Despite the agricultural depression there was money to be made from the soil, as seedgrowers showed. Around Coggeshall and Kelvedon there were many seedgrowers but perhaps the most unusual flowering of this Essex industry occurred at Saffron Walden. The town famed for the cultivation of the saffron crocus was equally famous in the middle of the 19th century for hollyhocks. Charlie Baron, a shoemaker, started it all. After a day bent over his last, he was glad to get out in his garden and tend his hollyhocks. He crossed and re-crossed his plants to produce wonderful new forms and shades of colour. He passed on his plants and his knowledge to William Chater, a professional nurseryman.

In 1847 Chater issued what was then the most comprehensive catalogue in the world of named varieties of hollyhocks. He revised it every year until 1873, when disaster struck – a terrible infection called simply the hollyhock disease spread through his nurseries and killed off every one of those rare varieties. Only the common, hardy plant survived, and the work had to be started all over again. But William Chater triumphed over tribulation. Before he died in 1885 he passed on his stock to Webb and Brand who could claim, in 1900, that they were the largest growers of hollyhocks in the world.

On May Day 1851, Queen Victoria opened the Great Exhibition, '. . . That wondrous palace of glass, within which is spread, as it were, a universe of human industry.' The list of contributions from the county is too long to reproduce here, but it included Bentall's agricultural implements made at the Maldon works, Coleman's of Chelmsford, Warren's of Heybridge and Jordan's of Billericay, all showing their latest implements. Fred Chancellor, the Chelmsford architect, showed his model of an improved farm and its yards, including a tramway for easy transport. Mr Mechi, celebrated innovative farmer of the Tiptree Hall estate, showed his 'Farmery' as an eight-feet-by-four model. All these exhibits demonstrated that modernised, mechanised farming was very much alive in Essex and there were many more examples of Essex art and craft.

All the while the last vestiges of the great Essex forest at Epping were being eroded. Trollope gives one reason for this in *The Three Clerks*, published in 1857: 'It is very difficult nowadays to say where the suburbs of London come to an end, and where the country begins. The railways, instead of enabling Londoners to live in the country, have turned the country into a city. London will soon assume the shape of a great starfish. The old town extending from Poplar to Hammersmith, will be the nucleus, and the various railway lines will be the projecting rays.'

It was not just the railway which threatened Epping forest, it was also the roads carved out of it by landlords greedy for the money to be gained from developing forest land into dormitory estates for London commuters. Some large land owners had used great tracts of the forest illegally, despite many local expressions of concern which eventually reached the ears of Parliament. One ordinary working man was the pivot of the movement which turned the tables on these developers. The full story has been told in *Essex Headlines*; suffice to say here that Lord Portman's Act of 1849 examined all the rights and claims concerning the whole of Waltham Forest, including the Hainault and Epping enclaves. Hainault, sadly, had so far deteriorated that its complete clearance was recommended and a vast estate of houses sprang up almost as thickly as the trees of the old forest. Epping's preservation was recommended, though in the 25 years before 1875 no less than 6,000 acres had been stolen from it by owners of neighbouring property.

In 1865 Thomas Willingale decided to carry on exercising the ancient right of lopping lower branches of trees for winter fuel. He climbed the fences behind which the forest had been enclosed, where trees had already been cut down on the line of proposed roads, and he was prosecuted, along with friends and relations who went with him. Some of them were imprisoned. Tom was considered too old for such treatment, but the owner of the land had him evicted from his cottage.

The mural in the lobby of County Hall, Chelmsford, depicting the official opening of Epping Forest and its dedication to the public by Queen Victoria in May 1882.

Other influential people took up his case, but poor old Tom died whilst it was in process. This case was the catalyst from which grew a public campaign, leading to the Epping Forest Act of 1871. Eventually, the City of London authorities bought out all individual owners through a local act of 1878. The Epping Forest Act of 1880 ensured the preservation of the forest under a ranger and conservators, on behalf of the City. Epping Forest was opened officially and dedicated to the enjoyment of the public at large by Queen Victoria in May 1882.

The Crimean War ended in 1855 and the valiant British Army was back in its barracks when Prince Albert visited Colchester the following year, to be entertained at the Moot Hall and taken on to review the combined militia of the Eastern Counties at Wivenhoe Park. In that same year Livingstone completed his epic journey across Africa. He was fêted as an intrepid hero. Whilst training as a missionary, he appeared in a less heroic guise. David Livingstone lived in a room above the archway to the Congregational Church in Chipping Ongar during 1840. He was sent out to Stanford Rivers to preach the sermon as part of his training.

He stepped up into the pulpit, gulped, and could only croak, 'Friends, I have forgotten all I had to say.' He hurried out of the church, covered in shame. Thankfully he was given a second chance.

The story of Victorian Essex is so full that events can only be sketched in. There is a wealth of information available in newspapers, public and private records in the county record office as well as resources of Essex County Library, all available to anyone interested in the further details of the county's history.

In 1880 the agricultural depression was biting hard, the result of five successive bad seasons and huge imports of wheat from America. The weather was the main topic of conversation. In January 1881, Grays Thurrock had four feet of snow in its High Street, and Essex felt the full force of a harsh winter. In 1884 an earthquake shook a large area of the county, radiating from its epicentre at Abberton. It still holds the record as the worst earthquake in British history. Shocks from it were felt up to 180 miles away. Nearly every chimney in Abberton was demolished. At Colchester the shock lasted eight seconds, and at Chelmsford five seconds. The damage in the immediate vicinity was considerable, but by the time the shock had reached these two towns it was only strong enough to shake buildings and give the residents a giddy feeling. Despite all the falling masonry at the epicentre not one person was seriously injured.

The outstanding event of 1888, for the nation in general and Essex in particular, was the passing of the Local Government Act. It established that the governing body of a county should be a council elected by the qualified inhabitants of that county. The first official meeting of the Essex County Council was held in the ballroom at the Shire Hall on 2nd April 1889. Only six months before the ancient county town of Chelmsford had at last received due recognition of its importance. The *Essex Weekly News* of 21st September 1888 reports: 'Today Chelmsford stands in the proud position of possessing a charter, granting to its inhabitants the highest form of local self-government. The new Borough has welcomed the actual receipt of the Charter in a manner which shows how great is the gratification amongst the inhabitants generally that its complete enfranchisement in matters of municipal administration has at last been effected. Wednesday, September 19th, 1888, will long be remembered as 'Charter Day' at Chelmsford.' But apparently there had been dissent; 'Although in the opinion of some the town never presented a brighter, cheerier aspect than on Charter Day, it cannot be denied that the decorations were not so general, nor the unanimity of the inhabitants so complete, as on the occasion of the County Agricultural Show last year.'

In 1897 Queen Victoria celebrated her Golden Jubilee. Buildings, clocks, horse troughs, drinking fountains and other memorials were erected in towns and villages throughout the county. There were exceptions. 'Chelmsford was unhappily one of these places . . . A section of working men and others were of the opinion that a treat to the schoolchildren . . . was not a sufficient or fitting recognition of the sixty years' reign . . . they demonstrated by indulging in a funeral procession wherein were carried black flags and a coffin which was supposed to contain 'remains' of the public library scheme.' The Act allowing local authorities to provide a library service dated from 1851, but Chelmsford did not get its library until 1906.

The 'New Century' from 1901 was greeted in the county newspaper with messages from county personalities, but the excitement was dimmed by the death of Queen Victoria on Tuesday, 22nd January. Her son, Edward VII presided over his first Privy Council on the very next day.

The most conspicuous feature in the history of Essex during the 19th century was the expansion of London into Essex, especially along the Thames where docks were built to accommodate the ever-growing seaborne trade. Factories were built in the immediate vicinity to take advantage of access to transport worldwide. As Kenneth Neale puts it, '. . . all the elements of industrial urbanisation . . . encroached on the woods and pastures of what ceased within the span of a man's life to be an authentic part of rural Essex . . .' Only at the end of the century, when modern local authorities were created, did this area receive the attention it needed in the terms of public health, adequate housing and the provision of suitable standards of water supply and other utilities.

The main area of expansion was at West Ham and along the banks of the Lea. Stratford and Silvertown were developed through the enterprise of the West Ham councillors, leading to its creation as a county borough in 1889. Ever outwards spread the tide of industry, with the Thames and the railways as the arteries of transport nationally and internationally. East Ham, Barking, Dagenham, Leyton, Walthamstow, Ilford, Romford; these and other pleasant old Essex villages were urbanised. East Ham was large enough to become an Urban District Council in 1894 and a county borough by 1915.

An interesting example of industrial development even further down the Thames was the establishment of Kynochtown, a place of which most Essex inhabitants have never heard. In 1895 the marshes which spread from Stanford-le-hope along the Thames to the brink of Holehaven Creek were wild and lonely. Then Kynoch and Company Ltd bought the 200-acre Borley Farm and built an explosives factory there, to meet the anticipated demand of the approaching South African war. It was an ideal site, surrounded by water on three sides – the Thames, Holehaven Creek and Shell Haven Creek, well away from human habitation and difficult of access by prying enemies of the state. Huts were erected to accommodate 600 workers, the men and women who made gun cotton, cordite, nitroglycerine and other explosives in huge quantities. Gradually a complete village was built to house the workers and their families. It included 40 houses, a school, an institute and a shop/post office. It was officially named Kynochtown on 18th November 1899. The school opened the following year and its head teacher Edwin Broad stayed until the end of 1927, even though the factory had been closed in January 1919. Cory Brothers took over the site in 1923, and Kynochtown became Coryton, the great oil refinery and storage depot.

An interesting account of the wide variety of industries established in Essex in the late 19th century is given in *Industries of the Eastern Counties Business Review* which states: 'The population of the county of Essex in 1851 was 369,318,. . . and at present numbers about 500,000. An enormous increase is constantly taking place in the number of

North Street, Romford, in 1910, still looking like a small market town. Its later development into part of the new Greater London Borough of Havering can be illustrated by the fact that every building in this photograph has been demolished.

156

inhabitants, this increase being chiefly on the side of the county adjacent to the Metropolis.'

The increasing concern over this period for the deprived and under-privileged is represented by the story of Dr Thomas J Barnardo who died in 1905. He lived at Mossford Lodge, Barkingside, within walking distance of the present Gants Hill roundabout. A guide book of 100 years ago tells us that the most important building in that hamlet was 'Dr Barnardo's Home for Destitute Girls. The inmates, numbering about 600, are accommodated in 30 separate houses arranged in a square. Others are in the course of erection. The matrons are chiefly ladies who voluntarily give their services.' That shows how famous these homes had become in a mere eight years, for they started as four cottages built in 1873 in the garden of Mossford Lodge. Dr Barnardo, born in 1845, was only 17 when he vowed to spend his life helping less fortunate people. In 1870 he had gained sufficient experience to open his boys' home at Stepney. In 1873 he adapted part of his own home, Mossford Lodge, to take in 60 girls. In the year of his death 1,300 girls were being brought up in 64 cottages spread around the Lodge's 300 acres. In his lifetime, Dr Barnardo was directly responsible for the rescue and the loving care of at least 250,000 children. His ashes are buried in the Children's Church of his village. He summed up the reason for his life's work with the observation, 'I have never seen an ugly child.'

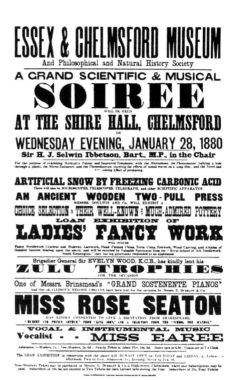

An increasing popular interest in all aspects of the arts and sciences is apparent from this poster for a Soirée at Shire Hall, Chelmsford in 1880.

13

THE EARLY TWENTIETH CENTURY

The world in 1906 saw social and natural unrest – a general strike in Russia, and San Francisco destroyed by earthquake and fire. In England the Liberals won a landslide election victory when a number of the new 'Labour' candidates were put forward for the first time. The women's suffrage movement was also stirring.

The big news in Chelmsford was the opening of the town's first public library on 3rd February 1906 by Lady Rayleigh. She also attended the Terling Flower Show to present that famous Essex gardener Ellen Willmott with a silver cup. A derelict wilderness in Warley is all that remains of a world famous garden that brought royalty on regular visits and attracted horticulturists from around the globe. Ellen came with her parents to live at Warley Place in November 1875. By 1898 she was left on her own in her beloved house and garden and spared no expense. Over 100 gardeners were employed. She had become so well known that the *Botanical Magazine* featured her in its Christmas number. No less than 40 plants are named after her or Warley Place. She spent all her money to keep the gardens going. As late as 1932 she was still sending out her valued seed list, naming over 600 plants. She died penniless on 26th September 1934 and the house and its lovely gardens were bought with the intention of developing them. Planning permission was refused in 1938; during the war bombs were dropped in a line across house and gardens and dereliction set in. At last, in 1977, the land was leased to the Essex Naturalists' Trust and volunteers worked at weekends to reduce the jungle to the point where a nature trail could be formed, showing wild and rare, cultivated flora growing side by side.

Chelmsford waited until 1962 for its first purpose-built Town Hall, yet Colchester had an impressive seat of government from 1902. Its decoration and statuary reflect the story of the town. Architect John Belcher used brick and stone to erect a rich 'Renaissance' style of building graced with a soaring tower. On the top of the tower stands St Helena, a statue in bronze representing the patron saint of the

A view of Colchester's Town Hall shortly after its opening in May 1902 by the Earl of Rosebery.

town. Below her, four ravens remind us that the ancient port of Colchester used the raven as its official seal. Lower down again are figures representing engineering, fishing, agriculture and the military – cornerstones of Colchester's economy. Nine stained glass windows continue the story, showing in glowing light a summary of the town's long and equally colourful history. Statues decorating the main building are of personalities connected with the Borough from Eudo, builder of the Castle in the 11th century to Samuel Harsnett, who rose from son of a humble baker in St Botolph Street to Archbishop of York in 1628. He died in 1631, leaving his library to the town of his birth. It is now in the care of the Colchester Library.

The rapid development of motor transport in Essex is demonstrated by the case of Thomas Clarkson. This bluff Lancashire lad, born in September 1863, was brought up in the Manchester area, a great place for a boy with a passion for engines at a time when steam was king and British-made machinery operated across continents. He became a

A Clarkson bus, probably a demonstrator (reg. no. F2582) first registered in 1908, shown outside the White Hart at Chelmsford in about 1910.

lecturer in metallurgy at King's College, London and in his spare time invented a number of steam driven systems, including a light steam car, patented in 1895. He went into partnership to develop these ideas, then, on his partner's death in 1899 he decided to go it alone, finding the premises he wanted in Chelmsford in 1902, on the site of an old iron foundry. His firm, Clarkson Ltd., produced a prototype chassis called 'The Chelmsford', designed to take eight passengers and their luggage over long distances.

It had few buyers, however, because petrol-driven internal combustion engines were then all the rage, though they were smellier, rougher and noisier than Clarkson's steam-powered machine. By the summer of 1905 nine models had been sold and were considered so satisfactory that orders came in from as far afield as Australia, India, New Zealand and Barbados. Clarkson designed a double decker steam bus for London routes and sold 37 to the two London omnibus companies. The Chelmsford factory was kept busy and hundreds of local people found employment there. When orders dwindled from 1908 Clarkson looked for other outlets, and found one in the Territorial Army. A trial was arranged at which the steam bus was to get troops from the Essex Yeomanry depot at Chelmsford to the banks of the Crouch in 1½ hours. On 6th December 1908, 128 men, accompanied by officers and journalists, 'embussed' at the local Territorial Headquarters in pouring rain. In one hour and seven minutes they were 'debussed' at Latchingdon, 14 miles away, and in one more minute they were formed up ready for action. The Commanding Officer, Colonel R B Colvin, was so impressed that he hired the buses to take the Yeomanry to camp. For this journey the buses were repainted with patriotic slogans like 'Wake up England'. But army bureaucracy was so slow that the factory nearly came to a standstill.

Clarkson's solution was to introduce his own London bus service, calling it The National Steam Car company. On Sundays his steam buses were used to take the great London public to local picnic spots like Epping Forest. By 1913 more than 20 buses were in operation and the company had taken over the bus services of the Great Eastern Railway operating out of the garage in Chelmsford, which consisted of one archway in the railway viaduct. By then the company was carrying 24 million passengers a year. In 1914 Thomas Clarkson was made chairman and managing director. Then things went wrong. He continued to research into steam transport while the board, seeing the odds against them, quietly expanded into petrol driven models. In 1921 the company parted with Clarkson, the Chelmsford works were sold, and the National Company and the 'Chelmsford' steam bus passed into history. Thomas Clarkson's epitaph was written long before his demise, in the *Gentleman's Journal*: '. . . It is such men as Mr Clarkson that have made the history of the advancement of the motor industry in England read like eleven years of miracles.' The designing and building of cars in Essex was what might be called a cottage industry long before Henry Ford arrived in Dagenham in 1925. In 1892 the Bremer car, named after its maker, was being produced at Walthamstow. In 1919 Mr Larcombe started producing his own car in a small garage at Margaretting. The place was burned down in 1929 and rebuilt. By then the huge factories with their assembly lines had taken over. The Larmar garage turned to making components for military equipment as the Second World War loomed.

One of the last men to be a coachman lived in Essex. He was J H Horton of Brook Street, Brentwood. He was driving a coach-and-four as a hobby when the new-fangled, infernal, internal combustion engine was driving horses off the road. In 1908 he declared publicly, 'You can have my opinions on roads and motor cars; they are pretty strong. There's no doubt that motors have come to stay but what I feel is that we country gentlemen should not have to keep up roads in our own district for motorists who come from a distance to tear up . . . Motorists should be much more heavily taxed – why should I have to pay a very much increased highway charge in order that I may make the roads better for people who come from all over the country, pay nothing for them, and also damage them severely?'

Seated high up on the box of his coach, Horton saw so much bad driving by these modern motorists. He said, 'Every now and then I met a motor cad seeking his own pleasure utterly regardless of everyone else on the road . . . I cannot say too strongly that this 20 mile speed limit must be preserved. If it is done away with we shall have men scorching through the place, subject only to the judgment of the police. Not ten minutes ago I saw a man come scorching through Brook-street wrapped in a cloud of dust, and going at least thirty miles an hour. It was quite impossible for anyone to tell his number owing to the dust.'

While Henry Ford was developing his 'Model T' in 1909, something much more important was going on in Colchester – everyone was rehearsing for the grand Colchester Pageant of 1909. What an amazing event it was when it was finally presented in June! The Earl of Warwick was the President of the Committee and the Master of the Pageant had a name to match that grandeur – Louis Napoleon Parker! It took over the whole of Castle Park and reflected in costume, in drama and in music the long history of this ancient Borough.

Crowds came to see it start with a meeting of the Druids, then the scene changed to the Roman invasion and the way in which they changed the town with their 'modern' improvements, including the great temple which is now the basement of the Castle Museum. On went the Pageant through the years to the awful siege of Colchester in 1648, and then to that proud building of the grand Town Hall in 1902.

Bleriot's aerial crossing of the English Channel in 1909 brought the minds of Essex folk to bear on the future rather than the past. A V Roe made the first British flight over the marshes beyond Walthamstow. Flying first came to Southend in 1910. There had been an approach from the London Aeroplane and Aerial Navigation Company a year before, with the idea of making aircraft there and testing them in flight, but finance was the stumbling block. Two other unsuccessful attempts were made at bringing Southend literally flying into the 20th century. Then, on 5th July 1910, it happened. A promoter arranged for the popular pilot George Barnes, of Brooklands fame, to come down to Southend and give a demonstration, in his monoplane, of this wonderful new art of flying. It took place on the football ground north of the town.

Barnes's plane was brought to Southend by true horse power, on a post-chaise, a four-wheeled cart. It was unloaded, assembled, wheeled to the centre-spot on the pitch and tuned-up for take-off. Next day the gates were opened and the 150 lucky people who had paid extra for the privilege were allowed to walk all round the plane for a closer inspection, before joining the rest of the audience in the grandstand. Barnes had announced that he would make a demonstration flight at half past six. Nature decided otherwise – the wind blew too strongly for the frail craft to get airborne. An hour later he tried again and rose just a couple of inches. He made one last effort to give the crowd value for money. He flew off into the gale, rose over the fence and landed 50 yards away, in the next field. It is hard to appreciate now what a miracle that first flight appeared to the hundreds of people gathered there.

Another crowd-puller at Southend that year was the Southend Beauty Show, then considered a national event, promoted by Mr Bacon at the Kursaal. It was probably the earliest example of protest against racial discrimination in Essex, for it was the first time a coloured lady had taken part. Princess Dinobulu from Senegal insisted, good-humouredly, that she be allowed to compete, and she won the hearts of the crowd, to the extent that one aspiring poet, Claude Greening, extolled her beauty in the local paper:

'Dinobulu, damsel dusky,
Dressed in taste and style,
Many a throat will be quite husky
Cheering your sweet smile!'

Prizes were awarded in three classes, according to hair colour, on the basis of the length of the audience's applause for each contestant. Despite that poet's enthusiasm, the Princess did not become the Queen.

The rural life of Essex at this time has been preserved for us in the writings of S L Bensusan, who wrote 60 books in as many years of his residence in what he called 'Marshland', which as C B Pulman puts it, '. . . shiftingly extends its unpegged boundaries through

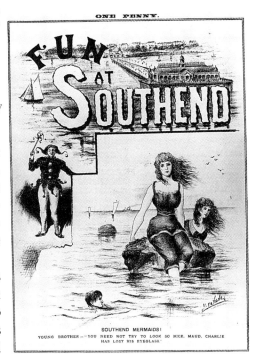

SOUTHEND MERMAIDS!
YOUNG BROTHER – "YOU NEED NOT TRY TO LOOK SO NICE, MAUD, CHARLIE HAS LOST HIS EYEGLASS."

Southend's increasing popularity as a holiday resort during the beginning of the century was helped by its successful exploitation of the bathing beauty show.

163

regions drained by Blackwater, Colne and Crouch, the inhabitants speaking in their own and ancient accents.' Bensusan was a London music critic and foreign correspondent who was told in 1886 that he had only about a year to live, and was recommended to end his days in the bracing Essex air, in calm rural retreat from stress and urban noise. In 1954 he was still writing. When Bensusan died in 1958 the *Times* obituary declared, 'Essex people and Essex ways were always the theme nearest this author's heart.'

It would be true to say that for all the nostalgic, simple happiness of village life there was very real poverty in the county. The workhouse was too often the last resort for the old and the oppressed. In 1910 'Christmas Day in the Workhouse' at Orsett, was reported in the local paper: 'In the entrance hall was a motto wishing all a happy Christmas, and also a well-laden Christmas tree. The various wards were all daintily decorated with mottoes, evergreens, coloured hangings etc. At 5.30 in the morning on Christmas Day the nurses ushered in the festivities by singing carols; a substantial breakfast being served at eight o'clock. At 9.30 there was a service in the chapel, hymns and carols were heartily sung. Tobacco and sweets were given out during the morning, and at 12.30 a sumptuous dinner was served. The fare consisted of roast beef (from cattle fed on His Majesty's Farm at Balmoral), mashed and baked potatoes, plum pudding and beer and mineral waters according to choice. Turkey was served to the sick. At 5.30 there was tea, which consisted of bread, butter and cake, with tea. A happy evening was spent in social enjoyment, singing and playing games, the inmates retiring to bed about nine o'clock ... Though it may be a misfortune to be in the workhouse, the lot of those living there is much preferable to that which thousands outside live, and Christmas Day as spent in the Orsett workhouse might be envied by many.'

The death of Edward VII and the succession of George V on 6th May 1910 would not have altered the plight or touched the lives of such people, but the sinking of the *Titanic* in the icy wastes of the Atlantic on the night of 14th April 1912 was on everybody's lips. Soon this disaster was overtaken by the cataclysmic horror of the First World War, proclaimed in August 1914. Many people had tried to alert Britain years before the conflict began. One of them was Claude Graham-White, an early aviator, who was determined to prove to the military that the aeroplane was the fighting machine of the future. From 1912 he barnstormed round Britain in his bi-plane with the message 'Wake up England' painted in large letters on the underside of the lower wing. He arrived over Clacton on 28th August, landed on the beach, then took off to put on his display. He swooped so low that he played leapfrog with rowing boats bobbing about on the briny, startling both occupants and onlookers, most of whom had never seen an aeroplane before. Graham-White told the press: 'Our people do not realise how backward we are in comparison with other countries and how our very existence will depend on our having a modern aerial fleet.' History proved him right.

Just before the war a most unusual hospital was founded in the heart of Essex. Early in 1913 a small group met to share their concern at the awful plight of British people who had caught leprosy during their service to their country in the outposts of empire. They raised enough money to set up a hospice, but owing to the uninformed fears and superstition of ordinary people, it was very difficult to find a site. One day these benefactors were driving through the narrow lanes east of Chelmsford when they lost their way. They knocked at the door of an old, dilapidated farmhouse to ask for directions. The farmer asked them in, gave them tea and asked what they were doing so far out in the country. They replied that they were looking for a property to buy, and he said 'I want to sell this place, why don't you look over it?' The group bought the 27 acres of land and the buildings that went with it, including the farmhouse, in the parish of East Hanningfield and the hamlet of Bicknacre, at a cost of £1,500.

After the local paper reported the plans to establish what they called 'A home for chronic disfiguring diseases and lepers' the local inhabitants, fearful that they might catch these diseases, called a public meeting at which it was declared that 'in the interests of the inhabitants, local dairy farmers, and owners of property, the matter should be reconsidered.' The group knew this would be the reaction wherever they went, so they had already obtained government approval, appointed two nursing sisters from Guy's Hospital and had admitted several patients to what was now called St Giles Home, secretly so that it could get started with the minimum of local hostility.

As the years passed and no-one caught leprosy, the village became very proud of the homes, run by the Brothers of Divine Compassion until 1936 and then by the Sisters of the Community of the Sacred Passion. The homes are no longer needed because modern medicine has beaten these diseases, but in their time they were visited by Her Majesty the Queen, Lord Louis Mountbatten, Princess Alexandra and the Queen Mother in 1974.

In July 1914 the county newspaper said in sombre tones, 'The blackest warcloud yet seen on the horizon of Europe ... is hovering over the land with dreadful menace.' Before the rain of destruction descended there was a lightening of the atmosphere with the enthronement of the new Bishop of Chelmsford, the Right Reverend J E Watts-Ditchfield, on 23rd April.

In August 1914 the Prince of Wales came to Brentwood to join the Grenadier Guards. Arriving at seven in the morning, his car passed through streets lined with Territorials sleeping on the pavement because the barracks were full of men called to the colours. By March 1916 the sad weekly Roll of Honour of Essex soldiers killed in action had grown to twelve long columns of very small print in the *Essex Chronicle*.

The six-volume story of the exploits of the Essex Regiment in the Great War was written by J H Burrows. General Sir Ian Hamilton declares in the foreword to the first volume: 'Essex is one and indivisible, so, too, are its people. Self-centred, self-sufficing, non-assertive, they are known to students, but – not as much as they should be – to fame . . . no one else, I believe, but Essex owns a Regiment which, in the old wars . . . was twice wiped off the face not only of the pay list, but of existence.' In his second volume John Burrows says of the 2nd Battalion, the Pompadours: 'It is a story which all Essex men and women will read with pride and mingled sorrow. Pride at what was accomplished by valour, constancy, steadfastness and cheerful endurance; sorrow that in playing so noble a part the County and the Battalion should mourn the loss of 1,457 officers and other ranks.' Whilst the Regiment's battalions went round the world to the theatres of war, the 8th Cyclist Battalion, who prided themselves on being a modern military development, an up-to-date unit, were disappointed that they were not chosen for overseas service. 'They were, at the outbreak of war, at once allotted the difficult and arduous task of watching the Essex coast. . .' The epitaph of the Cyclist Battalion must be 'They did their duty and they did it well.'

This was the first war in which civilians were terrorised indiscriminately by air attacks. In the early hours of 10th May 1915 a German Zeppelin attempted to drop its bombs on Southend, but the accuracy of the gunfire directed at the highly combustible airship forced it to move out of range beyond Canvey Island. Its Captain, Eric Linnarz, was so furious at being frustrated, for he was looking forward to a hero's welcome back in Berlin, that he ordered the Zeppelin to return to a high level over Southend, out of gunfire range. He took one of his personal calling cards from his pocket, wrote on it, 'You English! We have come and we will come again soon, to kill or cure' and threw it out of the Zeppelin. It was found and forwarded to the authorities; but the Zeppelin had also released its bombs, one in York Road, another at Cobweb Corner and a third in North Road where Mrs Whitwell was killed and her husband injured. Incendiaries set Flaxman's timber yard in Southchurch Road on fire. It was a frightening experience for unarmed, innocent and sleeping citizens.

Part of a platoon of C Company, 10th Battalion, Essex Regiment, taken in France, December 1915, during a respite from the trenches of the front lines.

The War Office, preparing for the protection of the country against this new aerial bombardment, set up airfields which allowed planes to patrol every inch of the coastline from Kent clear up to Scotland. To suit the capacity of the planes of the time airfields had to be spaced no more than 30 miles apart. That is why, in the early days of 1916, Stow Maries and Goldhanger had one of their larger fields taken over and closely mown. A big canvas hangar was put up, tents for housing the airmen soon sprouted along the edge and the planes came flying in. Only two planes were stationed at Stow Maries initially. They patrolled their sector from halfway to Goldhanger to halfway to Rochford, the neighbouring airstrips. By 1918 eight planes, some of them the famous Sopwith Pups, could be seen swooping low over the village as they turned in to land. When peace was declared the Goldhanger field was closed. Planes and personnel were transferred to Stow Maries, which boasted 24 aircraft and 300 staff, but it was all abandoned abruptly on 17th March 1919 when the whole squadron moved to Biggin Hill. The land quickly went back into cultivation and the airfield buildings were used as barns.

Hornchurch had an active aerodrome in both World Wars. On the night of 23rd September 1916 Lieutenant Sowrey took off from Hornchurch to intercept and destroy Zeppelin L32 on its way to bomb London. It fell in an appalling fireball, to crash one mile east of Great Burstead in open country. Its destruction took only two minutes. The remains, 250 yards long and 25 yards wide, spread across three meadows. Searchers recovered 28 bodies and they were first buried in Great Burstead churchyard, then transferred 25 years ago to the German war cemetery in Cannock Chase, Staffordshire for the convenience of German visitors. On the same night Chelmsford felt the impact of the first bomb to be dropped upon it from the air. It hit one of the cottages in Becket's Row, off Glebe Road, and passed right through the house to the kitchen where it ripped straight through a sofa and embedded itself in the earth beneath the floor, without exploding. The miracle was that only minutes beforehand a baby sleeping on that sofa was picked up to be fed by its mother. It was regarded as such an important event that an old photograph shows the cottage being guarded by four men – two

There was an outrage of revulsion at the German practice of dropping bombs on civilian targets from high flying Zeppelins. Here, in 1916, the first house in Chelmsford to be attacked in this way is being guarded by a constable, a 'special' and two military policemen.

military policemen, a constable from the Police Station and a wartime 'special'.

Essex men and women were involved in the naval sphere. Harwich was famous as the home port of the Harwich Force, two flotillas of cruisers and destroyers. The greatest story of individual bravery at sea must surely be that of Boy Cornwell, VC. Born in 1900 in Capworth Street, Leyton, Jack Cornwell left the council school in Walton Road to be a vanboy, but he wanted to be a sailor. The war gave him his chance. He joined the Royal Navy as a boy seaman and passed out as a first class boy on the light cruiser HMS *Chester*, which was involved in the terrible Battle of Jutland on 31st May 1916. His job was to act as sight setter for one of the big guns. Within minutes of the action his gun received a direct hit. Eight of the ten-man team were killed or injured. Jack's wounds were grievous, but the last order from the bridge had been 'Stand by your gun' and he continued to obey, terribly injured as he was. The Captain, high up on the bridge, saw this 16 year old boy standing there waiting for further orders and was so moved that he reported it to the Admiralty. Jack died two days later and was posthumously awarded the Victoria Cross. He is the youngest person ever to receive it.

When the possibility of peace shimmered over the shell-scarred fields of France the Essex men echoed the national cry of 'Homes fit for heroes to live in.' Though the dream went largely unfulfilled, the Housing and Town Planning Act of 1919 did make a great difference to that part of the county bordering London. London County Council was allowed to develop housing estates on land acquired in other local government areas. Becontree is a classic example of this process. Built in the countryside, it forms with Dagenham a huge housing estate, built between the First and Second World Wars, for resettling dwellers of east London. The land was acquired in the Dagenham, Barking and Ilford districts by 1922. In ten years more than 22,000 houses had been erected. By 1937 a stylish civic centre designed by E Barry Webber had been opened and has been much extended since then.

After the war a great feeling of relief and release swept the country. In our county that spirit was captured by the late Ursula Bloom in her volume of autobiography *Rosemary for Frinton*, where she lived as a young widow. She writes of famous people holidaying here at the seaside whilst their old haunts in Europe were still in chaos. A dance club called 'Victor's' was opened around 1920 and patronised in the season by people like Gladys Cooper, Ivor Novello, Lilian Braithwaite, Seymour Hicks and Joyce Carey. Another centre in Essex where the literati and the cognoscenti gathered was Easton Lodge at Little Easton, home of Frances, Countess of Warwick, whose association with Edward

VII, when he was Prince of Wales, caused such a scandal. In her *Life's Ebb and Flow*, published in 1929, she paints an amazing picture of culture in the countryside:

'In town one can choose one's friends, but, in the country, neighbours, often uncongenial, are thrust upon us. My neighbours have been a constant delight and inspiration. My mind flies, above all, to my tenants at the Glebe, to H G Wells and his wife and all their interesting entourage. In my "Laundry" live Philip Guedalla and his beautiful wife . . . at my Home Farm, Gustav and Isobel Holst have made a cottage into an abode of delight with an old barn for their music room . . . No more than a stone's throw from the Lodge the Horrabins rest from their editing of 'Plebs' and their political canvassing of Peterborough . . . In the old Easton Manor, where Edward IV and Elizabeth Woodville spent their protracted honeymoon, my youngest daughter Mercy, the wife of Basil Dean, entertains the stars of the theatrical profession at week-ends. The Park Cottage is the week-end haven of my son Maynard Greville . . . well-known writer to the 'Morning Post' . . . Further down the Park road lives Mr H A Gwynne, the editor of the 'Morning Post'. It was Mrs Gwynne who brought the ever-gracious personality of the late Ellen Terry into our gatherings at the Barn Theatre.'

The list of the famous goes on, to include finally, 'At Thaxted all the world knows of the rebel priest in his cathedral-like church of the Middle Ages, Father Conrad Noel, preaching the gospel of brotherhood and the championship of the oppressed.' He was a great friend of Gustav Holst, who lived in Thaxted from 1917 to 1925 and made the Whitsuntide Festival there an international event. Noel made many enemies through his intense socialist campaigning. In 1921 he hoisted high in his church the red flag of communism alongside the flag of Sinn Fein and the national flag of St George. Cambridge undergraduates came down to Thaxted in a body, borrowed ladders, tore down the two offending flags and hoisted the Union Jack. Noel's supporters ripped it down, burnt it and replaced their flags. The shouting and swearing which echoed round those ancient, sacred walls were repeated on Empire Day of that year when, in the churchyard, one of Noel's followers had his hat knocked off for failing to remove it when the *National Anthem* was played. The fighting spilled out into the street and cars and motor bicycles had their tyres slashed.

Sacrilege in Thaxted was balanced by reconsecration at Bradwell-on-Sea. The Romans had built a fort to protect the coast from raids by Nordic seafarers. When they left Essex around AD 400 it mouldered away, but when the new Saxon immigrants were converted to Christianity some 250 years later the missionary bishop, St Cedd, chose this place where he first came ashore as the site for the first Christian church. During centuries of neglect it was used as a lighthouse and ultimately as a barn. When its great religious antiquity was established, an anonymous benefactor paid for it to be restored as far as possible to the form of the original simple church. On 22nd June 1920 it was reconsecrated by the first Bishop of Chelmsford.

Another impressive building dating from the days of the Conqueror found a secure future in public hands at this time. Colchester Castle was not battered into ruins at the siege by Cromwell's army in 1648 – it had been crumbling away long before, because it was too big to be maintained even by the richest Baron. In the 17th century this sad-looking ruin had been sold to John Wheeley, on condition that he knocked it all down. He tried, even using gunpowder, for all that building material was valuable in a 'stoneless' county, but the bulk of that mighty bastion defeated him. The remains were eventually bought by Charles Gray, local MP and keen antiquarian, who appreciated the castle's place in the county's history. He spent his own money on ensuring that what was left was properly preserved. It then passed to Lord Cowdray who, in 1921, gave it as a gift to the Borough of Colchester, to stand as a memorial to all the people of Colchester who had served and suffered in the Great War. There could not be a better place in which to house the Colchester and Essex Museum.

The man most widely acclaimed in the history of Essex must surely be Guglielmo Marconi. A pamphlet issued in 1974 to celebrate the centenary of his birth recounts the development by him of wire-less transmission of messages over vast distances. By 1899 he was looking for premises to start commercial production of his equipment, and in that year acquired a former silk factory in Hall Street, Chelmsford. He was the major shareholder in the Wireless Telegraph and Signal Company which became Marconi's Wireless Telegraph Company in 1900 and The Marconi Company in 1963. The Hall Street works are famous as the first radio factory in the world. During the war, research and development was geared to the military effort. The regular service of broadcasting information and entertainment to the masses began in February 1922 from the Company's research laboratories at Writtle, after the Post Master General granted the first ever such licence. After broadcasting the death of Marconi on the morning of 20th July 1937 every wireless station in the world observed two minutes of silence – a gesture which is most unlikely ever to be repeated.

The General Strike was called in 1926. The county newspapers attempted to keep going, in much reduced form, to reassure their readers and to help preserve law and order. The *Essex Chronicle* was reduced to just four pages the following week, but the strike collapsed after nine days with just the miners staying out. People buying or borrowing books to escape the national misery found two Essex authors to entertain them. One was Warwick Deeping, who died in April 1950. His *Sorrell and Son* was published in 1925. He was born in Southend in 1877 in Prospect House, at the end of the High Street opposite the Royal Hotel, moving when he was still a small boy to Royal Terrace. He trained as a doctor but turned to writing novels, though at first he achieved scant recognition. But with a series of novels such as *Old Pybus*, *Roper's Row* and *Corn in Egypt* he won national acclaim.

Dorothy L Sayers's detective stories are still in print. She was born in 1893 and on her marriage came to live in 'Sunnyside', Newland Street, Witham. Many people remember her tubby figure bustling in and out of the shops there, where she was described as 'A loud, large lady, full of enthusiasm.' Millions of people all over the world have enjoyed reading those detective stories, starting with *Whose Body?* and *Clouds of Witness* in 1926. Lord Peter Wimsey, her aristocratic investigator, became so popular that he featured in more than a dozen novels up to 1937. Then she turned to plays and more serious works. She spent her very last moments in the Witham home she loved. On 17th December 1957, she suffered a massive, fatal, heart attack.

From Wimsey to windows and still in the neighbourhood of Witham – Silver End is a village which was built as a small estate for factory workers employed by Frank Crittall. By 1924 he had expanded his window-making business into three factories employing 1,600 people. Silver End began when Crittall built a special factory there to give employment to men disabled in the Great War. He went on to buy 220 acres of Boars Tye Farm and by 1930 had built a self-contained estate which included all the amenities then thought desirable, including a clinic, a cinema and a communal laundry. Even though they were then in their seventies, Frank and his wife moved to a new house overlooking the estate, to show their fellow-feeling. By then he was employing 5,000 people. He died in 1935, and his employees remembered him gratefully as the 'Guv'nor', strolling through the factory with a friendly word for all the staff he met. He was the first employer in the world to introduce a five-day working week, beating Ford's of Detroit by a good six months.

Ford cars first appeared for sale in England in 1903. By 1912 they were being manufactured in this country, at Manchester. It was the ever-increasing demand which caused the Ford Company to look for a larger site. So they came to Dagenham, on a 500-acre site beside the Thames where that famous breach had been made in 1707. In 1929 Edsel, son of Henry Ford, used a silver spade to turn the first turf on

The Ford factory at Dagenham, started in 1929. Remnants of the Dagenham Breach (see Chapter 11) can just be seen above the white building on the extreme left.

the day development of the site began. By 1931 production had been transferred from Manchester and 2,000 employees and their families were brought south to find new homes. In an early edition of the official guide to the London Borough of Barking, published in 1967, Ford's sums up its 'raison d'être':

'Since Ford came to Dagenham thirty five years ago, more than seven million cars, trucks and tractors have left our vast plant beside the River Thames. Some went by road and rail to home markets, nearly as many again to destinations overseas. These vehicles are a fine tribute to the people who built them.

For this reason there has always been a strong interdependence between Ford and the local community. We are proud to say that this relationship has been both a close one and a happy one.'

173

By 1931 flying was all the rage amongst rich young men. Towards the end of the year a group of these enthusiastic amateur aviators set up the Southend Flying Club, in a field in what was then the separate village of Ashingdon. They clubbed together to buy just one plane, an Avro 504K. Within a year they had enough members to move to the field at Rochford, which had once housed the pony racing track, and they traded in the Avro for a later model as well as buying two Tiger Moths and a Blackburn Bluebird. It became too big an operation for amateurs. Southend Flying Services was called in as a commercial firm to manage the club which from 1933 offered hourly trips to Rochester. This development was the spur that Southend Corporation needed to set up, in 1935, what we all know now as Southend Airport.

Stand on Maylands golf course today and you could hardly believe that this was once a busy aerodrome. It started in 1928 when a sloping field lying next to the A12 near Harold Wood was used by A H Matthews of the Essex transport company as the home for his first aeroplane (again an Avro 504K). By the following March it had become the base for one of those aerial circuses which took its four canvas and string machines on flying displays all over the country. E H Hillman offered a regular air taxi service from Maylands to Clacton and to Ramsgate. He organised the great Essex Air Pageant on 24th September 1932. The following year he started a regular service to Paris at a return fare of £5 10s 0d. It was a sell out and Maylands soon became too small. A new site was found at Stapleford Tawney in 1934. The Romford Flying Club stayed at Maylands and in 1940 all its aircraft and the hangars were destroyed by German incendiary bombs.

National news through the 1930s was of recession, depression and succession, leading to the resignation of the Labour government and rule by coalition under Prime Minister MacDonald. In June 1935 Baldwin succeeded MacDonald and in 1936, on January 20th, Edward VIII succeeded George V. He abdicated on December 10th, to be succeeded two days later by the Duke of York, George VI.

Through this difficult period the government put in hand a major programme of road improvement, to provide employment. The date 1932, inscribed in large letters on the railway bridge which carried the new Chelmsford bypass, can still be seen today, though that bypass has been swallowed by town expansion and another bypass takes the A12 well away from the town. Unemployment in Essex remained a problem until 1939, when the threat of war brought increased arms production and at the same time provided a doubtful but paid future for active men and women in war service.

14

THE SECOND WORLD WAR AND POST WAR ESSEX

Though the issue of the *Essex Chronicle* for 1st September 1939 was still talking of 'The Hope of Peace', the very next issue carried the banner headline 'UPHOLD YOUR KING AND COUNTRY' with the announcement that Britain had been at war with Germany since 11 am on Sunday 3rd September. Newsprint quickly ran short. On 29th December the *Chronicle* was reduced to four pages.

Harwich was involved in the war from the start, in an incident which could be said to have affected the course of the war. It was clear that Germany was developing the war at sea along two lines of attack, by submarines and by mines, but the Admiralty could not discover what weapon was used to blow four British ships out of the water. They tried a new tactic. When German planes came flying in low across Dovercourt Bay, the anti-aircraft guns were ordered to stop firing. Without the smoke and clutter caused by bursting ack-ack shells clouding the twilight of a November evening, observers spotted that from one plane an object was dropped into the sea. The area was calculated roughly and three destroyers were ordered to search it in daylight. One of them, HMS *Gipsy*, most tragically found that object. It was the Germans' new weapon, the magnetic mine. It was attracted to the metal of the destroyer, the charge was activated and the ship was sunk in a colossal explosion. Many of the crew were killed and injured. The wreck was raised and inspected with the greatest care. Thus the secret of the magnetic mine was discovered, and minesweepers were adapted to deal with them. The men of the *Gipsy* did not die in vain.

The first civilian casualties were in Clacton. A Heinkel had been laying mines off the coast to the north at midnight on 30th April 1940, when it met with a blanket of fog. It dived low to escape it and was spotted by an anti-aircraft gun battery which opened fire with such accuracy that it damaged the plane's rudder. It crashed against the side of a house, after knocking a number of chimney pots flying. Startled householders, peering out into the darkness of the black-out, had seen flames streaming from the hapless plane as it fell, but they were not prepared for the terrific explosion which rocked the whole town within a few seconds of the crash. One hundred and sixty people were injured. The four airmen were buried with full military honours in the cemetery, and children threw flowers on their coffins. One of the many wreaths was simply inscribed, 'With heartfelt sympathy from a Mother.'

In the same year, when Britain stood alone, the famous 'Few' operating from Hornchurch aerodrome wrote a chapter in the history of our county and our country which will never be forgotten. Where happy families now live in comfortable homes, the incredibly young fighter pilots sprawled on the grass waiting for the call to 'Scramble' against an enemy far superior in numbers. For a month from 12th August 1940, the Hornchurch fighter squadrons were on continuous alert. They destroyed 164 enemy aircraft, but many of those brave young men were also lost. The aerodrome itself was attacked no less than 23 times during the war. It was not until 1962 that this famous aerodrome was closed and developed as a housing estate. The old station badge is kept safely by Havering council – a small symbol of a great fight for freedom.

On 23rd August, 1940, John Ockelford Thompson, Mayor of Chelmsford and one of the owners of the *Essex Chronicle*, wrote a letter to the editor for insertion in his own paper. It said: 'May I draw attention to the Flight of Fighters Fund? No words can describe the gallant and noble hearts of our airmen. Their work is an epic in history . . .' He chaired a meeting to start this fund, aiming to raise £15,000 to purchase a flight of fighters for the RAF. This was his seventh year as Mayor of the County Town, having first taken on the task in 1916. He was liked by everybody in the many spheres in which he moved.

From the date of that letter in August we move on to the night of 13th October 1940. The obligations of the day were over. Alderman Thompson and his wife were in bed after a pleasant evening with their son Lt. Col. T U Thompson and his two children, who had called to stay the night on route to their own home. That night a German bomber dropped its load of bombs indiscriminately over Chelmsford. One high explosive bomb hit the house, and the Thompson family was wiped out. It was like slamming a book closed when it was only half read. The wartime generation of Chelmsfordians never got over it. Let this one tragedy stand for all the deaths by bombing which Essex people suffered throughout the war, from incendiaries which caused terrible fires along the Thames and up the coast, to the deadly rockets which fell silently from the sky to cause appalling damage and casualties.

One relic of that time has been restored. At Blake Hall, Bobbingworth, the 25 acres of gardens are a big attraction for summer visitors; but for

Service officers and a government official inspect the remains of the crashed Heinkel at Clacton on 30th April 1940, and survey the destruction caused by the mines it was carrying.

those whose memory stretches back to that war there is a special spot, just one room in the graceful Queen Anne house. This room rises from the ground floor right up to the roof. It was specially converted at the beginning of the war to serve as the operations room for No. 11 Group Fighter Station, based at North Weald aerodrome.

At ground level a vast plotting table filled the room. From galleries rising round the walls a team of 'controllers' watched all aircraft passing into and out of the area by looking down at the table where women of the WAAF used long pointers to move arrows representing the planes. From this room the call went out to North Weald to scramble our fighters to take on the might of the German air force. It is kept as it was as a memorial to those brave young airmen.

As well as being bombed, civilians suffered great restrictions on their travel. Not only did everybody have to carry an identity card with them at all times, but also, for the three years from 1941 to 1943, no unauthorised person could approach within ten miles of any part of the Essex coast. This wartime bureaucracy gave rise to some strange situations. For example, Colchester was included in this ban, but people from Nayland were allowed to go into Colchester to do their shopping. When one lady rang the police to ask if she could go to Colchester to visit the library they acted strictly according to the book. 'No', they said, 'You can go round the shops, but you can't go in the library'! That was a minor problem compared with the bombing, the rationing, the disruption of travel, the blackout and so many more annoyances and discomforts suffered by Essex people right until the day the final wartime restriction was removed on 3rd July 1954.

The entry into the war of the United States made a huge impact on the Essex landscape. The first airfield built by the Americans in this country was Andrews Airfield at Great Saling. The army engineers came in July 1942 and finished the job in a back-breaking, record-making year. They named it after one of their famous air force generals. The hardcore came from the ruins of the London blitz and the speed of construction was achieved by two shifts of men working day and night.

There are at least 15 memorials erected in Essex to the memory of people killed in air accidents or in the course of enemy air attacks. At Boreham, where the Ford Company now runs its rally centre, there is a simple brick pillar with a plaque remembering that this was once US Army Air Force Station 161. At Bradwell-on-Sea a memorial, built in 1987, shows a twelve-feet long, cast iron model of a Mosquito plane nose-diving into the earth, with an inscription remembering the 121 men from the allied air forces who 'left this airfield to fly into the blue forever.' Very few people realise that the south porch of the Cathedral at Chelmsford was rebuilt as a memorial to the American forces who served in Britain for three years from 1942. In Colchester a seat has been placed in Trinity Square as a memorial to the airmen who occupied several bases around the town.

There were many unsung Essex heroes and heroines. In July 1942 bombs were dropped on Witham station. The newspapers were not allowed to print a report until six months later, when they told of the complete destruction of the main line and severe damage to the station and its sidings by bombs which left craters 25 ft wide and almost as deep, yet such was the spirit of the people that it was repaired and ready to receive trains just four hours and twelve minutes later. Then there was that terrible blow just before Christmas 1944 when a V2 rocket fell beside the Hoffmann ballbearing works in Chelmsford. Forty workers, mostly girls, were killed just 15 minutes after they had been singing carols with the Salvation Army Band.

The war in Europe ended on 8th May 1945. The General Election of the following July was a landslide victory for Labour, but a lot of servicemen and women were still thousands of miles away from their Essex homes, fighting the Japanese until the atomic bombs brought their capitulation on 18th August. From 1947 onwards the coal industry, the railway network, electricity and gas supply were nationalised. In that same year the floods in England on March 15th were the worst ever recorded. As far as Essex people were concerned those floods were nothing as compared with the flood damage caused by the abnormally high tide which by 2 am on 1st February, 1953 had overwhelmed more than half of the 308 miles of embankments and sea walls which protected Canvey Island in particular and the permanent homes, caravans and chalets in general which had sheltered so confidently behind what was thought were impregnable defences. One hundred and nineteen people died in those cold, February waters which covered some 50,000 acres and flooded more than 12,000 homes. Countless farm animals were cut off and drowned in that relentless rising of the tide. The whole story has been told magnificently and in detail by Hilda Grieve in *The Great Tide* published in 1959 by Essex County Council.

Canvey Island was one of the hardest hit areas. From 1.30 am three times the sea swept clear across the island. By nightfall the gallant rescuers had evacuated 10,000 people and every house had been checked and its inhabitants taken to safety. Families living in wartime Nissen huts at Great Wakering saw the flood creep up to roof level as the rescue services struggled to extricate 110 people from their perilous predicament. The most touching story of these Essex floods came from Canvey Island. Baby Linda Foster, just eight weeks old, was found floating on the flood in her carry-cot. She had been wrapped up carefully by her mother, but when Mr and Mrs Foster got to the front door of their bungalow they found the flood already too deep. Mr Foster held his wife above his head until he drowned and was washed away. Mrs Foster held the baby's carry-cot above the water as long as she could, then she sank exhausted. Baby Linda survived, to be brought up by her grandparents.

By 1957 all the sea defences had been repaired and rebuilt to a higher level, to ensure that such a horrendous calamity would not occur again. The defences on Canvey Island have been raised again in recent years to compensate for the installation and the raising of the London Flood Barrier if ever the need should arise.

In 1953, on June 2nd, Queen Elizabeth II was crowned in a grand ceremony, seen for the first time on television. Her father George VI had died on 6th February 1952. The *Essex Chronicle* ran to 32 pages

179

Harlow, designated as a New Town in 1947, was designed by Sir Frederick Gibberd who spent the rest of his life in the town that he had created.

on 12th June as a 'Coronation and Essex Show Souvenir', announcing proudly, 'As the premier county newspaper which is today reporting its seventh coronation and has faithfully served a wide readership in nine reigns, we have the great honour and privilege to acclaim Queen Elizabeth II.'

The happy relationship between Essex people and their American allies lasted long after the end of the war. In June 1957, for example, a crowd of no less than 46,000 attended the open day at Wethersfield air base. At the same time a new age was dawning – an age of the peaceful use of atomic energy – and after four and a half years of building work it was announced in June 1961 that Bradwell Power Station had reached the final testing stage. It was designed by Maurice Bibb and was fully commissioned in 1962. Thousands of local people and tourists have visited the Station.

At the same time as the nuclear power station came on stream, Essex

County Council was looking for suitable premises for the newly formed Essex University. Hylands House at Widford, near Chelmsford was passed over in favour of Wivenhoe Park. The original Georgian house, seen in a painting by Constable, was incorporated in a large mansion designed by Thomas Hopper for the Rebow family in 1846. Today the feature which greets the visitor on his approach is the group of severe yet lofty residential blocks.

When the war ended a renewed interest was taken in the housing of the expanding number of people working in London who wished to live on its Essex edge. As the *County Handbook* says: 'As the accessibility of Essex has improved, more and more people have moved into the county, both from London and other parts of Britain. Managing this population influx has been a major concern for many years. The task of the county planners was eased when, in 1946, legislation made it possible to house people and industry in purpose-built, self-contained communities, or New Towns.'

A hundred years ago Basildon was not even a parish, just a collection of houses in the area called Laindon-cum-Basildon. The New Town of Basildon saw its first new house completed in 1951. In 40 years well over 30,000 such houses have been built in an enlarged area which embraces the old towns of Billericay and Wickford. Local employment has been encouraged, with around 600 industrial units totalling in excess of ten million square feet. The shopping centre draws custom from far beyond its boundary. Yet in the country park of Langdon Hills, in Norsey Wood, Billericay, or in the Wat Tyler Country Park adjoining the creeks of the Thames estuary, one could be a million miles from the throbbing life of the New Town. This has not happened overnight. Norsey Wood was not acquired by the authority until 1976. Now it is a nature reserve maintained by volunteers under the aegis of the Council.

Harlow's development starts with its designation as a New Town on 25th March 1947, covering just over 6,000 acres and a population of 4,500. By 1951 twelve industrial firms were in business there and the late Hugh Dalton, Minister of Town and Country Planning, had opened the first residential tower block. In the next five years 7,000 dwellings and 70 factories were built and the town had its own newspaper, the *Harlow Citizen*. In another five years all the public services and utilities were fully in place in new premises. The best sports and recreational facilities in the county were available by the time that 'First Night' was celebrated at The Playhouse Theatre in 1971. The New Town came of age in its 30th year when government approval was given for the transfer from the Development Corporation to the locally elected Harlow Council of the last of the houses built under its jurisdiction.

The Harlow District Council had been in operation from 1974 when, under local government reorganisation, it took over from the Harlow Urban District Council set up in 1955. The assumption of control from the Development Corporation was slow and smooth.

Whilst Essex countryside was being developed '. . . primarily to help in dispersing the people and industries of London and other congested cities', a Royal Commission set up in 1957 was considering the problems of administration caused by the ever-increasing urbanisation of London's environs. Its deliberations resulted in the Local Government Act of 1963 and the setting up of the Greater London Council from 1965, when those parts of Essex contiguous to London were absorbed into five Greater London Boroughs. They represented six per cent of the land of the county, but more than 50 per cent of the population.

Dagenham and Barking were united as Barking, with a population of about 180,000. It is now totally developed and urbanised, but is still looking for a corporate identity. Havering combined the borough of Romford and the urban district of Hornchurch. The new name was the ancient name for a royal manor in this area, with special rights and privileges still observed until 1892. Unlike Barking, Havering has been fortunate in that many parks and open spaces have been preserved and the new Borough still includes a good deal of real countryside. Its character is as much residential as commercial and industrial.

The Borough most crushed in the capital's suffocating embrace must be Newham, lying on the bank of the Thames with the Roding separating it from Barking on the east and the Lea dividing it from Tower Hamlets on the west. There is no country air to be breathed in the old urban areas of East Ham, West Ham, Little Ilford and a small part of Barking and North Woolwich. It has long been an area of heavy industrial production of gas, chemicals, sugar and, later, electrical components.

Redbridge meets the county border to the west above Newham and Barking. It reaches far into the old Essex countryside to include Ilford, Wanstead, and Woodford. Its name recalls an old bridge, replaced many times, which carries Eastern Avenue across the Roding as it bisects the Borough.

Waltham Forest, home to around a quarter of a million people has been described as rising '. . . in distinct tiers from the winding banks of the Lea to the tree-clad horizons of the Epping Forest ridge.' Much of it has been developed to accommodate industrial sites and housing estates. Towards Chingford there is still some evidence of the big houses which once looked over farmland dotted with hamlets. It was the coming of the railway that made Leyton, Chingford and Walthamstow so convenient for work and business in the capital.

The Thurrock Lakeside Regional Shopping Centre: multi-million pounds' worth of American-style shopping mall and leisure complex.

Despite the wholesale transfer of such a large proportion of its population, Essex was still under pressure to provide more and more housing in keeping with modern standards and expectations. Essex County Council answered the challenge. It decided that an area of the parish of Woodham Ferrers, called for convenience South Woodham Ferrers, '... constituted an area where housing could be provided without materially restricting the availability of open space for amenity and recreation' – to quote the 1976 edition of the *County Handbook*. County officers established the title to the land; organised additional access to the site with bridges over the railway, and planned the service requirements in advance of building on a green field site as large as any undertaken at that time. 1,300 acres would be covered with houses, shops and public amenities, to serve a population planned to rise from a nucleus of 4,000 to an ultimate 18,000. The 4,000th new house was occupied in March 1988.

The 1990 *County Handbook* stated 'Today the building continues. The Chafford Hundred development at Grays Thurrock, begun in 1988, is the biggest housing project of its kind currently under way in Britain. About 5,000 houses are planned, as well as new shops, schools and a railway station. Nearby, the Thurrock Lakeside Regional Shopping Centre, also begun in 1988, is a multi-million pound development which will provide an American style shopping mall and leisure complex, the largest in Britain.'

County administrators also had to handle the reorganisation from 1st April 1974 of local government. Overnight all the existing boundaries as well as the more recent county borough, urban district and rural district divisions were replaced by a new County Council and 14 District Councils. With the population now standing at more than one and a half million, that is a heavy responsibility.

One of the main reasons for the continuing growth in population, and thereby industrial and topographical development, is the vast improvement in the road system during the post-war years which has put Essex not just on the doorstep of London but practically into the hallway. The most important element in the road system was the completion of the M25. In an interview in May 1985, the County Treasurer declared, 'It has changed the nature of the County, opening south Essex up for business and industry.' It was the M25 which made the development of the old quarry area around Thurrock, some 2,000 acres, a viable proposition.

That ancient highway, the A12, driving north east from London right through the county was looking like a wriggling worm even on pre-war maps, because, by the end of 1934, bypasses had been proposed or completed around Barking, Chelmsford (replaced by a much wider loop in November 1986), Colchester and several towns and villages in between. It has lost its premier status in the county to the M11, the first section of which was opened in June 1975 and the second, southwards to London in 1977. In 1980 a northern section towards Stumps Cross was completed, thus giving a quick passage through Essex to Cambridgeshire. In the other direction this motorway, like the A12, joins the M25, completed in sections from south to west from 1982 to 1984, to take the Essex motorist round London to every point of the compass. On southwards, the M25 leads to the tunnel under the Thames from Purfleet to Dartford, known as the Dartford Tunnel.

The value of such a tunnel had been seen as early as 1935, when Essex and Kent County Councils had agreed to a joint venture, but the Minister of Transport vetoed the plan, 'on grounds of national economy.' Postwar increase in road traffic made the tunnel a priority. It was opened on 18th November 1963 and attracted so much traffic that a twin tunnel had to be constructed alongside it and opened on 16th May 1980. The pressures of rapidly increasing population and individual car ownership, together with the transfer of goods from rail to road haulage

A new Essex landmark – the Queen Elizabeth II Bridge over the Thames at Dartford, opened by the Queen in 1991.

in juggernauts meant that Dartford Tunnel was soon notorious for traffic tailbacks. So a new toll bridge across the Thames was built on a line similar to that of the tunnels by a private company. It was opened on 30th October 1991 by Her Majesty the Queen at a special ceremony. It was then the longest cable-stayed bridge in Europe, rising to a height of 70 yards above the Thames. Its four lanes all lead south, allowing the two tunnels to provide four lanes for traffic heading north.

Railways, on the other hand, have been very much slimmed down. Numerous lines have been closed. The Kelvedon, Tiptree and Tollesbury – the old 'Crab and Winkle' line opened so hopefully in 1904, closed to passengers in May 1951 and to goods in October 1962. The Maldon, Witham and Braintree Railway opened late in 1848 and extended from Braintree to Dunmow and Bishops Stortford in 1864. The Braintree-Witham section escaped the Beeching 'axe', but the line in the other direction was closed in stages, until the final shut-down on 17th February 1972. The Elsenham and Thaxted Light Railway, opened in 1913, closed in 1953; there is now hardly a trace of its existence. The Wivenhoe and Brightlingsea branch line did not reach its century; it opened in April 1866 and closed in June 1964 – doomed by car ownership. In 1865 the Saffron Walden Railway only went from Audley End, on the main line. It was extended to Bartlow a year later. Not a great success, its busiest years were during the last war, servicing the great Walden petrol store. After the war, business fell away drastically and it was closed at the end of December 1964.

The Colchester, Stour Valley, Sudbury and Halstead line struck off from the main line at Marks Tey and ran twelve miles to Sudbury in 1849; in 1865 it was further extended into Suffolk. The great feature of this branch was, and still is, the 355 yards long Chappel viaduct. The line closed on 1st January 1962. The Colne Valley Railway began operations in 1860 with more declines than inclines on its chart of fortune. The Second World War provided the high point on that chart – in the summer of 1944 some 7,000 wagonloads of bombs were carried to the American-built airfields either side of the line. Then came the slow decline to closure in April 1965. Yet the old locomotives can still be seen there, under steam, because volunteers have reconstructed a mile-long section of the line out of Castle Hedingham station, where engines and rolling stock are on display. At Chappel and Wakes Colne station, the other end of the line, there is another railway 'museum' offering 'steam-up' days. The Tendring Hundred Railway lines flourished under nationalisation, but the Wivenhoe and Brightlingsea branch line, opened in 1866, was not successful. Yet, despite being badly damaged by the great flood of 1953 it was fully restored, to be patronised by less than 600 daily users until it was closed on 15th June 1964.

The full story of the development of railways throughout the county has been told by D I Gordon, in *The Eastern Counties*, volume five in the *Regional History of the Railways of Great Britain*.

One of those early airfields, built in 1942 for American B46 bombers, continued after the war, slowly building up business as a civil airport. On 24th March 1964 it was chosen provisionally as the site for London's third airport. Despite the strongest local protest, and after an enquiry into the feasibility of a scheme to develop a huge airport on the Maplin Sands off Foulness, Stansted remained the firm favourite. In March 1991 the Queen opened an ultra-modern complex worlds removed from the ex-army hut which served as the first terminal of Stansted Airport.

From the air Essex is still very much an agricultural county, though the outlook for farmers as they come increasingly under directives from European bureaucracy is rather bleak. Fields lying fallow by financial arrangement between government and farmers remind one of the earlier periods of agricultural depression when tenant farmers were bankrupted, crops were not worth growing, and fields became wildernesses where rabbits proliferated.

Some of the set-aside fields are being developed as leisure parks and golf courses, and there is growing awareness of the county as a tourist centre. The County Council is actively promoting Essex through the British Tourist Authority, under the *Development of Tourism Act 1969*.

Although as late as 29 July 1988 the Queen opened the new County Hall in Chelmsford, there is in the area of government planning, a definite whisper of a new attitude to local government; a situation in which the county council would be abolished and the 14 districts would be entirely responsible to, and depend upon, the grants and approval of central government. The Chief Executive of Essex County Council said in *Essex in Action* in October 1991, 'This is a time of great change, with a proposed review of Local Government. We face any review with confidence in the knowledge that the more people who know about what we do, the better able they are to take part in the debate on the future of government in Essex.'

In 1992, a thousand years after those Norsemen came ashore and did battle with the Saxons at Maldon, another invasion took place – a friendly, festive occasion when Americans returned to the scene of their service in Essex in the Second World War 50 years before. They found their way through town and countryside now almost unrecognizable, to stand in a field, by a house, even in a factory, on the exact spot where they had come back 'home' to Essex after missions against the Nazi war machine. They saw more clearly than the inhabitants the amazing changes made in Essex in 50 years.

In looking back at the story of our county through 10,000 years we gain the inspiration to make our contribution to the life of the county, defending its environment and its way of life until another generation takes up the challenge.

Bibliography

Addison, William *Essex Heyday* Dent, 1949

Anglo-Saxon Chronicle Ed. Dorothy Whitelock, Eyre & Spottiswoode, 1961

Bayne, A D *History of Eastern England* MacDonald, 1873

Bensusan, S L *A Marshland Omnibus* Duckworth, 1954

Briggs, Nancy *Georgian Essex* Essex Record Office, 1989

Brown, A F J *English History from Essex Sources, 1750–1960* Essex Record Office, 1952

Buckley, D G ed. *Archaeology in Essex to AD 1500* The Council for British Archaeology, 1980

Burrows, J W *Essex Units in the War, 1914–1919* 6 vols, 1923–35

Campbell, James, General ed. *The Anglo-Saxons* Phaidon, 1982

Chapman, John and Andrè, Peter *A Map of the County of Essex from an Actual Survey Taken in 1772–3 and 1774*

Christy, Miller *Durrant's Handbook for Essex* Simpkin Marshall, 1887

Clark, Sir George, ed. *The Oxford History of England* Clarendon Press, 15 vols, 1937–1965

Coller, D W *The People's History of Essex* Meggy and Chalk, 1861

Corke, David *The Nature of Essex* Barracuda Books, 1984

Crouch, Marcus *Essex* Batsford, 1969

Darby, H C *An Historical Geography of England Before AD 1800* CUP, 1936

Defoe, Daniel *A Tour through the Eastern Counties of England*, 1772

Douglas, David C *William the Conqueror* Eyre & Spottiswoode, 1964

Drury, P J *Excavations at Little Waltham 1970–71* The Council for British Archaeology, 1978

Edwards, A C *A History of Essex* Phillimore, 4th Edn., 1978

Essex Chronicle (Under various titles from 1764 to date.)

Essex County Council *County Handbook*

Essex County Standard, formerly *Essex Standard*, from 1831

Essex Record Office *Essex 1066–1901: A series of illustrated booklets* 1963–1966

Essex Review 1892–1957

Essex Weekly News from 1862

Excursions in the County of Essex Two volumes, Longman, 1819. (No author is shown – the preface is signed 'The Editor'.)

Federation of Essex Women's Institutes *The Essex Village Book* Countryside Books, 1988

Fraser, Antonia, ed. *The Lives of the Kings and Queens of England* Weidenfeld and Nicolson, 1975

Grieve, Hilda *The Sleepers and the shadows* Essex Record Office, 1988

Harrison, William *The Description of England* 1577

Hopkins, Matthew *The Discovery of Witches* 1637

Hull, M R *Roman Colchester* 1958

Jarvis, Stan *Essex Pride* Ian Henry, 1984

Jarvis, Stan *Hidden Essex* Countryside Books, 1989

Jarvis, Stan *The Rivers Chelmer and Blackwater* Terence Dalton, 1990

Jarvis, Stan *Smuggling in East Anglia 1700–1840* Countryside Books, 1987

Jarvis, Stan *A View into Essex* Terence Dalton, Revised Edition, 1990

Kelly's Directories Ltd. *Directories of Essex,* 1845–1937

Leland, John *Itinerary* ed. L Toulmin Smith 5 vols., 1907

Martin, G H *Colchester: Official Guide*

Morant, Philip *History and Antiquities of the County of Essex* 1768

Neale, Kenneth *Discovering Essex in London* Essex Countryside, 1969

Neale, Kenneth *Essex in History* Phillimore, 1977

Oman, Sir Charles *The Great Revolt of 1381* OUP, 1906

Perry, John *Account of the Stopping of the Dagenham Breach,* 1721

Pevsner, Nikolaus *The Buildings of England: Essex* 2nd edn., 1965

Pigot's *Directory of Essex,* 1839

Reaney, P H *The Place-names of Essex* CUP, 1969

Reaney, P H *Essex* Republished 1970

Salzman, L F *England in Tudor Times* Batsford, 1926

Smellie, K B *A History of Local Government* Allen & Unwin, 1946

Stenton, F M *Anglo-Saxon England* OUP 3rd edn., 1971

Taverner, James *An Essay upon Witham Spa,* 1737

Trevelyan, G M *English Social History* 2nd ed., 1946

The Victoria History of the County of Essex In progress from 1903

Warwick, F E *Countess of Warwick. Life's Ebb and Flow* Hutchinson, 1929

Wright, Thomas *The History and Topography of the County of Essex* 2 vols., 1831 and 1835

Young, Arthur *General View of the Agriculture of Essex,* 1807

Index

192